PENGUIN BUSINESS
DATA SCIENCE: A BEGINNER'S GUIDE

C. Raju is a full professor in the quantitative methods and operations management area at the Indian Institute of Management Kozhikode (IIMK), India. He had a two-decade-long academic career with the University of Mysore from early 1985 till July 2004. In this period, he held different positions as lecturer, senior lecturer, reader, professor, public relations officer and director, Center for International Programs. He was invited as a visiting professor by Armstrong Atlantic State University, US, from January–February 2002. During his sabbatical (2002–03), he associated himself with CAMO Software as a domain expert for the multivariate analysis statistical software called Unscrambler. He served as a professor at the SDM Institute for Management Development from 2004 to 2005 and taught quantitative methods, operations research and marketing research. He also worked as the chief executive officer of JSS Education Foundation Pvt. Ltd., Mysore, from November 2005 to May 2009.

Professor Raju steered the MBA programme under executive education at IIMK to a global level. He served as dean of administration and development, dean of extension programmes, and dean of executive education at IIMK from 2017 to 2021. He played a key role as nodal professor, Indian Institute of Management Amritsar, from October 2017 to November 2019 in mentoring students.

He received his bachelor's, master's and PhD degrees in statistics from the University of Madras. He was a Council of Scientific & Industrial Research (CSIR) research fellow. His doctoral work was in the area of acceptance sampling. He has published several articles in international peer-reviewed journals. His research interests include acceptance sampling, multivariate data analysis and PLS regression.

Professor Raju has a passion for statistics and enjoys teaching the subject to people from different educational backgrounds.

T0026605

Celebrating 35 Years of
Penguin Random House India

ADVANCE PRAISE FOR THE BOOK

'As research, including that in the social sciences and humanities, is becoming more and more data-based, at least basic knowledge of statistical theory and application has become necessary for all researchers. However, many scientists, especially in the life sciences and social sciences, are usually terrified of mathematics and statistics. This book, with simple explanations and examples, provides an excellent source to introduce fundamental statistical concepts even to a layman and enthuse one to go for more advanced knowledge'—Mewa Singh, PhD, FASc, FNA, FNASc, FNAPsy, distinguished professor for life and SERB Distinguished Fellow, Institution of Excellence, University of Mysore

'This is a wonderful book that focuses on our understanding of data science with practical, simple examples. The concept of a safe zone across industries with interesting examples and different definitions of a safe zone makes it easy to understand. All concepts related to data and data science are explained well'—Darshan Danda, manager, technical support engineering, Salesforce

'*Data Science: A Beginner's Guide* lucidly describes statistical concepts. Its everyday examples provide a feel for complex topics. Its simplicity nudges the reader to finish the entire book in one go. The book is a must-have for beginners, practitioners and anyone who works with numbers to refresh core concepts. I enjoyed every bit of reading it'— Subbarao Vemula, lead programme manager, Otis Elevator Company

'Dr Raju, with his versatility in statistics and business, explains statistical concepts in an easy-to-read manner in this book. I had the pleasure of reading it. The book exposes you to the concepts of statistics and everyday observable data without expecting any prior knowledge from you. It is also a refresher on the basics of statistics and data. I advise reading it at leisure and enjoying the learning'— Aprameya Paduthonse, cloud, data and software development professional, Virginia USA

'"Humans are born with knowledge of data science". With the very first assertion that it makes, the book immediately hooks the reader and promises to be a captivating read. And it doesn't disappoint! A fantastic read, the book's ability to delve into concepts that are fundamental for anyone starting on the path of data science makes it the ideal must-read beginner's guide. A timely tonic, this book needed to be written!'—Professor V. Charles, PhD, PDRF, FRSS, FPPBA, MIScT; professor and director of the Centre for Value Chain Innovation, CENTRUM PUCP, Peru; associate professor for AI for business; director of PGR Studies, University of Bradford, UK; special chair professor, Ming Chuan University, Taiwan

'This is a good book for managers and students to understand data science and its applications. It provides a big-picture look at data science with simple examples. To quote an instance, production lead-time analysis and effect of order cancellation are explained through simple histograms and box plots. I appreciate Professor C. Raju for explaining regression, binomial and Poisson distribution with simple cases'—Rajeev Ranjan Kumar, cloud virtual desktop delivery head, Wipro Limited

'. . . an insightful guide full of important information for those of us who want to enter the data science world, especially ML [machine learning] and AI [artificial intelligence]. Dr Raju has nicely articulated data insights and their applications and explained descriptive measures, probability and probability distributions, inferential statistics, and regression concepts with examples. I highly recommend this book for beginners'—Abhay Kapale, cyber security specialist master, Deloitte

'This beginners' guide to data science is just what one would need to simplify and relate to data. This is a book for everyone and not just for data nerds. The focus is on covering the essential quantitative techniques and using everyday activities as examples, making all the concepts simple to understand. It covers diverse foundational concepts ranging from scales of measurement to variables and probability, all in a way that you could relate to. The examples picked from real-life scenarios like brushing teeth, baking bread, etc. make quantitative ideas easy to understand and apply. Would highly recommend it to anyone with an interest in anything to do with data'—Garima Dhamija, co-founder, Salto Dee Fe Consulting

'Professor Raju does a good job introducing statistics to any reader. It is nice to see how common life experience is used as a medium to introduce the concepts. It showcases the journey of data and relationship building, and leads the reader to realize business value'—Naveen Mekala, director, product ownership, Adidas, Amsterdam, the Netherlands

'Statistics used to be my biggest fear, so much so that my sympathetic nervous system would switch sides from fight to flight. I still remember attending your first class, [it] was the last day of my fear of this subject. Your natural humour mixed with concepts, which you explained by correlating to real-life scenarios made this subject fun to learn'—Vaibhav Tyagi, corporate trainer, NIIT Limited

Data Science:
A Beginner's Guide

C. Raju

Series Editor: Debashis Chatterjee

PENGUIN
BUSINESS

An imprint of Penguin Random House

PENGUIN BUSINESS

USA | Canada | UK | Ireland | Australia
New Zealand | India | South Africa | China | Singapore

Penguin Business is part of the Penguin Random House group of companies
whose addresses can be found at global.penguinrandomhouse.com

Published by Penguin Random House India Pvt. Ltd
4th Floor, Capital Tower 1, MG Road,
Gurugram 122 002, Haryana, India

First published in Penguin Business by Penguin Random House India 2023

ISBN 9780143461722

Typeset in Sabon by Manipal Technologies Limited, Manipal

www.penguin.co.in

To
my wife Vidya
and
children Ashwini and Vikram

Contents

Notes by Series Editor   xi

Preface   xiii

Foreword   xvii

Introduction   xxi

1. Humans Are Born with the Knowledge of
   Data Science   1
2. Data and Descriptive Measures   14
3. Probability and Probability Distributions   47
4. Inferential Statistics   103
5. Regression—Building Relationships   186

Notes by Series Editor

Data science is a perfect blend of 10 per cent math, 20 per cent statistics, 30 per cent common sense and 40 per cent application knowledge. While you can learn math and statistics, common sense and application of what you have learnt accrue with experience.

This introductory book on data science triggers the innate knowledge you have. With straightforward real-world examples and applications, it takes you on a path that may have seemed difficult. It endows you with a holistic and flawless understanding of the fundamental principles required to build a solid foundation in data science.

In this book, Professor C. Raju arrives at the simplicity on the other side of complex mathematical mazes. Refreshingly clear, enriched with an easily graspable narrative and laced with humorous examples, this work is a signature expression of a very popular teacher.

—Debashis Chatterjee,
director, IIM Kozhikode

Preface

The greatest compliment I received from one of my students was that she had learnt quantitative techniques so well that she will remember it clearly enough to teach her grandchildren. She went on to say in her letter that she was able to explain probability even to her arts graduate landlady because of the way it was introduced to her by me. What more can a teacher ask for? So, when several students and working professionals who were pursuing an MBA through executive education suggested I put my teachings into a little book as a light read that would help people grasp statistics, I paid heed. Inspired by such recommendations, as well as my experience with industrial applications, and conversations with academic acquaintances and members of my own family who have chosen to work in this burgeoning field of data science, I decided to publish a book of this nature.

The intent is to remove the hesitation of many in taking up statistics and data science on the assumption that the same is filled with complex mathematics and computations. In this book, the concepts, including probability, are made simple with real-life examples so you can explain the same to your grandchildren as well as grandparents and have a conversation around these topics with anyone at any time. Data science is explained from the perspective of interpretation and application rather than from a purely mathematical or engineering perspective.

The explosion of data science aids every industry in leveraging data to improve sales, reduce carbon emissions, optimize supply chain and logistics, and better engage with customers and clients. Not only data scientists but also business leaders must understand and leverage data science to succeed and sustain in business. Data science finds application in every domain—finance, retail, marketing, supply chain, e-commerce, logistics, last-mile delivery, medicine and regulatory bodies, to name just a few.

This book is a quick read for anyone who wants to get into the field of data science with confidence.

I would like to take this opportunity to record my sincere thanks and appreciation to all my friends, academic peers, industry leaders, and importantly, my students, who have been part of my conversations and provided feedback at every stage of writing this book.

—C. Raju

Foreword

We now know scientifically that every organic form, shape and colour in nature is the result of a pattern. Whether this mathematical formula dictates the formation or only explains the nature around us is a matter of philosophy, but we all agree on the equivalence of organic forms and the underlying math.

We all have 99.999 per cent of the same DNA as our animal ancestors, and these five 9s carry all the intelligence and advancement achieved so far by our race. Yet, we know that the breakthrough for humans evolving from animals came through that 0.001 per cent aberration in the copying of DNA, which led to breakaway leaps of growth.

Similarly, we often see in corporate life that companies strive to identify and scale 99.999 per cent of their DNA to make their processes repeatable and of high quality. This has made many good companies great and also helped consumers benefit from economies of consistent quality from producers. We also see certain breakaway growth companies focus all their energies on the 0.001 per cent chance and fundamentally transform industries, such as Apple, Uber, etc. More so now in the face of a rapidly increasing pace of change in environments and markets, where consistency could become a synonym for momentum, or in other words, the ability to change direction at speed.

This makes us think about what human excellence is, to build a solid 99.999 per cent or to make the 0.001 per cent completely transform the old 99.999 per cent. Thankfully, you have a path for both in statistics—to bring explainability, to algorithmize the 99.999 per cent, and hence scale it for competitive advantage, and to identify the 0.001 per cent change in light of the rapidly changing extraneous environments and markets, and to identify opportunities and harness them before your competitors.

In this book, Professor Raju has beautifully illustrated and elaborated on the central tendencies of human behaviour, manifested fully through data, with several relatable examples from our daily lives, at home and work. Professor Raju has introduced contemporary statistical concepts on how to capture core behaviour into a mathematical equation, or what we often called explainability. You can explain human behaviour, a business or the flight of a missile through a mathematical equation, which could also allow you to forecast the outcome. Professor Raju has also succinctly explained how one can forensically look at 'discrepancies' in data, which are often also sources to understand changing behaviour at the cutting/leading edge of the curve, ahead of time. All extremely useful techniques, almost mandatory for every modern manager to be aware of if not to use in managing the environment.

I want to congratulate and thank Professor Raju for this wonderful gift to academia and the industry, for putting in simple terms the importance of statistics and data and introducing not just the why but also the how of harnessing data for increased competitive advantage. The book is a holistic yet simple read, and despite being an advanced practitioner, Professor Raju has managed to keep the book an interesting and insightful read all the way.

Happy reading!

Sumit Dhar
SVP corporate strategy
Genpact, The Netherlands

Introduction

The science of statistics, currently known as data science, is the only subject that is closely associated with human life. Each and every activity of human life can be explained and managed well with statistics. For example, if one defines the inhalation-and-exhalation cycle (the intake and expulsion of air during respiration) as a breath, the number of breaths one can take in a minute can be explained with a probability distribution. Likewise, calorie intake, calorie burnt, time spent on social media, sleep hours, blood pressure, pulse rate, income and expenditure, sales in terms of physical and monetary volume, forecasting and prediction of business and economic indicators etc., can be studied with the help of statistics.

This book walks the readers through the basics of data science that helps build a strong foundation to understand and apply the same in all practical situations. The book has an introduction and gradually builds on the different concepts to give the readers a continuous flow and flawless understanding of the data science. Each concept has been explained in simple language and appropriate practical examples. Using appropriately chosen data sets computation of various statistics using Excel is explained.

Chapter 1 takes the readers through the real-life situations and introduces how data science revolves around daily activities. Data that originates naturally creates a safe zone automatically and hence informs users on how to respond when an out-of-safe-zone signal is flashed.

Chapter 2 introduces the concept of data and different descriptive measures that are used to understand the data. The different descriptive measures are naturally born out of our desire to seek data. This creates interest among the readers to appreciate the concepts of data science as natural entities and that formulae are mere representations of the concepts. As a process of understanding the descriptives hidden in the data, data visualization, cleansing, presentation and analytical methods are explained with appropriate real-life data.

In Chapter 3, probability and probability distributions are explained. The word 'random' is explained through some real-life examples. From random, gradually the concepts of probability, marginal, joint and conditional probabilities are explained. Rules of probabilities such as union, intersection and multiplication are explained through examples. The probability of an experiment is a number between zero and one that represents the relative likelihood of the occurrence of the event. A probability of zero means that the event is impossible, while a probability of one means that the event is certain to occur. Probabilities are usually assigned to events based on their nature. If the outcomes or events are equally likely to occur, then the probabilities are assigned equally to all the outcomes or events. This method is called classical probability approach or theoretical probability approach. Another approach of assigning probabilities is known as the empirical approach or frequency approach. Empirical probability is based on the frequencies of occurrence of an event out of total frequency. The probability is defined as the ratio of the frequency of the occurrence of an event of interest to the total frequency. A subjective approach is used based on the assignor's (subjective) judgement.

A random variable is a real valued function that assigns numerical values for all possible outcomes of a random experiment. Every outcome of a random experiment has an associated probability. The random variable is discrete or continuous depending on whether the sample space is discrete or continuous. Probability distribution of a random variable is a mathematical expression that distributes probabilities to all possible values the random variable can take. It is used to model and analyse random phenomena such as climatic pattern, stock prices, medical diagnostics and voting pattern, etc.

The probability distribution is discrete or continuous depending on whether the random variable is defined on discrete or continuous sample space. Discrete probability distributions are used to model events where the outcomes are defined over a discrete sample space, such as flipping a coin or rolling a die. Continuous probability distributions are used to model events where the outcomes are defined over a continuous sample space, such as height or weight of individuals in a population.

The expected value of a random variable is a measure of its central tendency, and is defined as the sum of the possible values of the random variable weighted by their respective probabilities. It is used to describe the long-term behaviour of a random variable, and is a key concept in probability theory and statistical analysis. The concept of expectation is the key aspect in life insurance and is used in deciding the premiums.

There are a few basic probability distributions of discrete and continuous random variables that are widely used in practice. Bernoulli, binomial and Poisson distribution under discrete distributions, and normal and exponential distributions under continuous distributions are widely used in practical situations. Bernoulli distribution is used when there are only two values the random can take, such as 'yes' or 'no'. The binomial distribution is obtained when a Bernoulli experiment is repeated n times. The binomial distribution is a discrete probability distribution that is used to model events with two possible outcomes, such as flipping a coin or rolling a die. It is characterized by a probability mass function that describes the probability of each possible outcome. The Poisson distribution is a discrete probability distribution that is used to model events that occur at random intervals, such as the number of phone calls a call centre receives in a given hour. It is characterized by a probability mass function that describes the probability of each possible number of events occurring.

The normal distribution, also known as the Gaussian distribution, is a continuous probability distribution that is commonly used to model natural phenomena such as height, weight, speed, distance and examination scores. It is characterized by a bell-shaped curve, with most of the data falling within one standard deviation of the mean. The exponential distribution is a continuous probability distribution that is used to model the time between events that occur randomly, such as the time between earthquakes or the time between customer arrivals at a store. It is characterized by a probability density function that describes the probability of each possible time interval. Theoretical distributions help modelling and analysing real-world phenomena and make predictions about future events.

Chapter 4 discusses the inferential statistics. In most of the practical situations, the population is either large or unknown. Studying about the parameters of the population becomes difficult, expensive or sometimes impossible. In such situations, the population parameters are usually estimated using the sample. The primary purpose of inferential statistics is to study a portion of the population (sample) and generalizing the results of the sample to hold good for the entire population. This is done by estimating some of the population parameters with a certain level of confidence or precision.

There are two types of estimation of parameters namely, the point estimation and the interval estimation. Point estimation involves providing a single value as an estimate of the unknown parameter, while interval estimation involves providing a range of values (interval) which is supposed to include the unknown parameter with a probability statement that serves as the confidence coefficient. Interval estimation involves constructing a confidence interval, which is a range of values that is likely to contain the true population parameter with a certain level of confidence. The confidence intervals are mostly based on normal distribution or t-distribution. This is based on meeting the requirements of the assumptions on normality or not. As in most situations the population is unknown, the use of t-distribution is usually recommended. Confidence interval is the basis for predictive analytics.

A hypothesis is a statement/assertion/claim/ assumption about an unknown population parameter the validity of which can be tested. Testing of hypothesis is used to determine whether a hypothesis about a population parameter is supported by the available evidence from sample. The process of hypothesis testing involves several steps, including formulating the null and alternative hypotheses, choosing a significance level, collecting data, calculating test statistics, determining the p-value, making a decision and interpreting the results. Depending on the nature of the parameter on which the hypothesis is made and the assumption of the underlying probability distribution, either a test based on normal distribution of t-distribution is used.

Chapter 5 deals with regression that is used to study the relationship between variables. Linear regression is used to model the relationship between a dependent variable and one or more independent variables. In simple linear regression, there is only one independent variable, and the relationship between the dependent variable and the independent variable is assumed to be linear. The goal of simple linear regression is to estimate the slope and intercept of the linear equation that best describes the relationship between the variables. In multiple linear regression, there are two or more independent variables, and the relationship between the dependent variable and the independent variables is assumed to be linear. The goal of multiple linear regression is to estimate the coefficients of the linear equation that best describes the relationship between the variables.

Logistic regression is used to model the relationship between a binary dependent variable and one or more independent variables. The dependent variable can take only two values, usually coded as zero or one, representing a binary outcome such as success/failure, yes/no or true/false. Logistic regression has many applications, such as predicting the likelihood of a customer purchasing a product based on their demographic characteristics, predicting the likelihood of a patient developing a disease based on their medical history and predicting the likelihood of a loan default based on the borrower's credit score.

In conclusion, this light introduction to data science is aimed to provide a solid foundation for understanding essential concepts through the use of numerous examples and simple language. By breaking down complex ideas into easily digestible components, it will hopefully make data science more accessible and engaging for readers of all backgrounds. As one continues to explore the fascinating world of data science, these fundamental concepts serve as building blocks, enabling one to tackle more advanced topics with confidence. Ultimately, this book not only demystifies data science but also inspires a lasting appreciation for the insights and knowledge that this powerful discipline has to offer.

1

Humans Are Born with Knowledge of Data Science

When a child is born

Imagine a situation when a child is born in a hospital. Soon after the baby is delivered, the mother and child are brought to a room. The mother is still recovering from the trauma of delivery, tired, and is lying on the bed semi-conscious or unconscious. As is usual medical practice, the baby is swaddled and placed in a cradle. This is to keep the baby at the ideal temperature, which is the same it was enjoying while in its mother's womb for nine-plus months. This is an amazing scene to remember and ponder. When suddenly for some reason the temperature in the room changes, becoming either warmer or colder, one can see that the baby feels uncomfortable. The baby makes all sorts of facial expressions and tries to move the cloth tightly wrapped around its body. It tries to adjust to the new temperature. When it cannot do so, the baby cries. By crying, the baby tells the people around that it needs help to cope with the new temperature as crying is the only language the baby knows at the time of birth. If the father of the baby is the watchdog in the room, he will try to pacify the baby by swinging the cradle or singing a song. The moment the baby hears the singing, it will cry louder. On hearing the loud cries, a nurse will run into the room to help. If the nurse is experienced, she will keep the baby by the left side of the mother without disturbing the sleeping mother. The baby will instantly stop crying. This is because the baby feels it is in a safe zone. The feeling of a safe zone is important. What is a safe zone?

It is not difficult for most of us to guess/understand the reason behind this. We are all aware that the baby was in its mother's womb for nine months and hence is well-tuned to the sound and rhythm of the mother's heartbeat. The baby, which is now placed by the left side of the mother, hears her heartbeat and understands that it is in the safe zone. One may be surprised to learn that the baby will not stop crying if placed by the side of any woman other than the mother. What happens here is that the baby:

a) can understand the numbers behind the heartbeat, which may be measured in decibels;

b) can identify the rhythm of the heartbeats that it had been listening to during the nine-plus months in the mother's womb; and

c) can compare and contrast these heartbeats with those of other women.

Here is the fact. The baby understands the heartbeat in terms of numbers and can differentiate the heartbeat of other women from the heartbeat of its mother and by identifying the heartbeat of the mother, feels that it is in a safe zone. Thus, at the time of birth, the baby knows its mother, while the mother has to be told this is her baby. This is the beauty of the science of statistics or the so-called data science, which is now understood in applied terms such as six-sigma. Hence, it is seen that humans are born with knowledge of data science. This gift of birth is unlearned during the process of growth, and when necessary, everyone starts relearning it.

The scientific facts are:

a) When a change in temperature is felt, the baby attempts to adjust to the new temperature, showing facial reactions and trying to move the swaddling. The baby is checking if the temperature is around the target temperature, plus or minus a tolerance. When it fails, the baby cries. This is the same as in the six-sigma customer-supplier situation. When the specifications of product quality parameters in terms of target and tolerance are not met, the manufacturer cries.

b) When the baby is placed beside the mother, the baby listens to the mother's heartbeat. It measures the heartbeats in its way and finds that the heartbeats are around the target, plus or minus the tolerance. The baby feels that it is in a safe zone and hence stops crying. This is the natural phenomenon followed in the manufacturing process in industries. For every quality parameter, the manufacturer arrives at a target value plus or minus the tolerance called the specifications, in agreement with the customer's requirements, and maintains his manufacturing set up so that the manufactured products meet specifications. If the measured parameter value of a product fails to meet the specifications, it will be termed a non-conforming product.

c) The baby will not stop crying when placed beside other women because it knows it is not in the safe zone as the target and tolerance are not met.

Cooking a roti

Consider cooking a roti, a staple of Indian food. Among those familiar with Indian food, if asked what the shape of a roti is, the answer will be 'round'. Usually, if you ask why the roti is round, no one knows the answer. They will probably say that generationally, we have been seeing the roti made in a round shape, from grandmother to mother, and mother to daughter, and so on. The actual reason why the roti is round lies in the science behind cooking it. There are two reasons for it. The first reason is psychological, that the round is the most pleasing geometrical shape for the human eyes. The second important reason is physics. Heat spreads uniformly across a round object and therefore the roti gets cooked uniformly and hence consumes less energy. It may be fun to see the first roti made by someone, which may look like a world map. Although disappointed with the shape of the first roti, on successive trials one is able to make a round roti.

After that, the rotis are always made round, of a particular diameter, and uniformly thick. If fifty rotis are made at a time, it may be observed that all those fifty rotis will be of the same weight (target weight plus or minus one or two grams), same diameter (target diameter plus or minus one or two millimetres) and same thickness (target thickness plus or minus a fraction of millimetres). It should be noted that rotis are made without a prototype but only keeping in mind the round shape. How does one always end up making round rotis that are similar in diameter and thickness? Whatever may be the process followed in making round rotis (rolling, pressing, etc.,), it is the innate knowledge sitting inside one's head that guides and directs the trial-and-error process so one successfully arrives at round rotis. The innate knowledge one is born with aids in fixing our own standards in terms of target and tolerance for the diameter and thickness, that decides the roundness of the roti and checks for confirmation at every trial by increasing or decreasing the pressure, rolling, etc. For each parameter of a roti, one creates a safe zone, and staying within these safe zones results in rotis that one is satisfied with.

Brushing one's teeth

The daily activities of humans have instances of the safe zone theory. The first activity of a typical day is brushing one's teeth. For how many minutes does one brush one's teeth? The answer would be for between two to five minutes. If one records the time taken to brush one's teeth over a month, the thirty measurements would have an average value and a tolerance around the average value creating a safe zone of time taken to brush teeth.

Calorie intake

Measurements in calories of daily food intake, both total for the day as well as individually for each meal, during breakfast, lunch, dinner, snacks, etc., do have target values (usual consumption) and tolerance. Being in the safe zone of calorie intake will help one stay healthy.

Sleep duration

Sleep duration is an important health factor. Sleep is widely recognized as an important component of mental, emotional and physical well-being. Healthy sleep is characterized by an adequate duration of sleep. If the sleep time of individuals during the night is recorded for thirty days, it may be seen that there is a safe zone using which one may understand and monitor the status of health.

Commute time

Commute time to the workplace from the residence is an integral part of everyone's daily schedule. An assessment of this commute time is important during the initial days of work, after which it becomes a routine. The routine commute time has a safe zone, which is usually involuntarily maintained.

Retail stores

Retail shopkeepers always try to be in a safe zone concerning fast-moving consumer goods (FMCG). They keep updating the inventory/stock of their products so they don't run out of them.

Pharmacy

Pharmacies are mostly associated with a few doctors and hospitals in the proximity of the shops. They have a fairly good idea of the medicines prescribed by the doctors as marketed by the medical representatives. Most pharmacies try to be in a safe zone by keeping an inventory of frequently prescribed medicines. This helps in a greater supply chain and avoids reverse supply chain activities.

Sports

In the new era of data science, almost all sports have become analytics-oriented. In tennis, badminton, cricket, football, etc., the players learn to place themselves in a safe zone rather than in defensive/offensive/aggressive plays. Availability of data helps players learn the analytics of a game and work towards improving their game. This helps the players overcome the emotional aspect of the game. Players can come out of their safe zones and exhibit the power of play, leading to unexpected results. Will there be stories in the future such as those of Steffi Graf, Martina Navratilova, Stefan Edberg, Ivan Lendl, Chris Gayle, Brian Lara, Sachin Tendulkar, Brett Lee, Shoaib Akhtar, Viktor Axelson, Kento Momoto, Tai Tzu-Ying, Akane Yamaguchi, Chen Yufei, Pele, Diego Maradona, Lionel Messi, Cristiano Ronaldo, Johan Cruyff, etc.?

Credit cards and fraudulent transactions

The use of credit cards has been increasing in India with a growth rate of over 12 lakh users a month and an average of Rs 6.7 crore in outstanding every month. While this makes credit cards a good business for financial institutions, with it comes the risk of figuring out who to issue credit cards to, what limits to offer a specific person based on their profile and most importantly, to avoid fraudulent transactions that can take place through a variety of mechanisms. Financial institutions spend heavily to ensure all transactions operate within a customer's safe zone, that is, typical transactions with similar spending patterns, such as at their regular petrol stations, usual Starbucks outlets and so on, and focus on transactions that fall outside the safe zone, which can indicate fraudulent transactions due to compromised personal and financial information.

Walk rate in retail business

Every retail store is always looking at signals to see how they can maximize their revenue. Understanding what consumers want and prefer and what core categories/brands are deemed essential becomes crucial to understanding what drives their revenue. It is also important to understand what is the safe zone of operations, which sometimes is to ensure a particular brand is stocked (for example, IDFresh batter, without which a proportion of customers might walk out without shopping for other items—this is known as walk rate in retail business analytics), sometimes entails removing certain items from a category to make space for other items to ensure that the sales performance of the category improves and shelf space is not reduced, while sometimes the safe zone is just ensuring that Sona Masuri rice and tur dal are priced at Re 1 less than the competition.

Personal genomics

23andMe is a personal genomics test that is commercially sold. It is a reputable DNA test that provides people with information about their ancestry. You send in a spit sample and the company will compare your DNA to a very large genome pool, based on which it provides detailed insights into your lineage. However, 23andMe has recently expanded to also provide predictive health services. Their first step in doing this was offering a genetic weight report. The company employed machine learning to analyse the effect of more than 300 mutations on a person's weight. They also analysed various lifestyle effects such as sleep deprivation or stress, and their impacts on the expression of certain gene pathways that might contribute to a person's weight. This analysis is done by tracking shifts metabolic hormone levels, factors that commonly cause these levels to oscillate out of the safe zone are catalogued. By using unsupervised machine learning to recognize patterns between lifestyle, nutrition and genomics data, 23andMe can send a consumer an extensive report on what factors in their life might be contributing to their weight from just a spit sample and a lifestyle questionnaire. Since their first endeavour into health analysis, 23andMe has developed a health kit that provides genomic reports on a predisposition for genetic illnesses, carrier statuses, wellness factors and phenotypic traits.

Pharmacogenetics

Pharmacogenetics is a fast-growing field focused on using genomic information to inform medical decisions, specifically medication decisions. Take the prescription of the anaesthetic codeine for example. Normally, only 10 per cent of codeine present in the body is converted into morphine, and this ratio is used to inform what dosage to give a patient. However, some people carry multiple copies of genes that encode the enzymes involved in the metabolism of codeine. These patients are categorized as ultra-metabolizers, and they can metabolize up to 75 per cent of the codeine present in their system. While a standard dose of codeine for a patient with a normal metabolism would have a simple anaesthetic effect, for an ultra-metabolizer, the amount of resulting morphine produced could be lethal. Like this, thousands of genes affect how different chemicals are processed in our bodies. Pharmaco-geneticists are utilizing machine learning to accurately identify and analyse the complicated network of enzyme pathways in our bodies. In order to do this, pharmaco-geneticists must determine whether various genetic mutations can cause a person's enzyme and hormonal levels to fluctuate out of the safe zone. This effort to develop genetic tests that could help doctors be more informed of each patient's metabolic characteristics will allow for precise medical decision-making and in turn, save lives.

InnerEye

Analysing medical imaging is a skill that can take doctors years to master in medical school. There are many cases where tumours have been overlooked or misdiagnosed due to how challenging it can be to interpret medical imaging. Microsoft has an ongoing project called InnerEye, which focuses on using computer vision and machine learning to analyse 3D medical images. This application determines whether the orientation or gradation on a scan falls within a safe zone, if not these irregularities are flagged. InnerEye is already being utilized in a hospital in Cambridge where it has shown 90 per cent reduction in the time clinicians take to plan radiotherapy treatments.

Thus, safe zones are always in our minds. Someone who is out of their safe zone feels uncomfortable and seeks the reason behind the deviation and attempts to rectify it. What is observed is data, and what is inferred from data is information. As one seeks to identify deviations, one realizes that the data the human brain can remember and interpret is limited. There is much more data in this universe beyond what human sensory organs can assimilate. The data can be related to each other in unimaginable ways, which can be beyond human perception. Fortunately, in today's world, computers can supplement human brains. Computers can accumulate large amounts of data and synthesize it in predictable ways. This field is called data science. Data science helps in one's quest to find safe zones.

2

Data and Descriptive Measures

This chapter introduces the concept of data and different descriptive measures that are used to understand the data. The different descriptive measures are naturally born out of the desire of human beings wanting to know some information from the data. This creates interest among the readers to appreciate the fact that the concepts of data science are natural and formulae are mere representation of the concepts. As a process of understanding the descriptives hidden in the data, data visualization, cleansing, presentation and analytical methods are explained with appropriate real-life data.

Nomenclature

Population The collection of conceivable units in a given region of the study. A conceivable unit is a unit that gives the desired information. Only such units that provide the information desired can form the population.

Sample   A representative portion of the population. The sample is expected to contain all information available in the population.

Parameter   A function of all observations in the population, usually a descriptive measure derived from the population.

Statistic   A function computed from the sample, usually a descriptive measure derived from the sample. This function need not be based on all observations in the sample.

Data

Data is both singular and plural. In the singular sense, it means a given fact (derived from the Latin word datum). In the plural sense, it means a collection of facts. Data is classified into qualitative (categorical) and quantitative (numerical). When the data is expressible in numerical terms, it is quantitative. When the data is not expressible in numerical terms it is qualitative.

Variable

For convenience, the general characteristic being observed is considered a variable. Depending on the data, the variable under study may be qualitative or quantitative. A qualitative variable is expressed in terms such as beauty, colour, taste, hygiene, etc. A quantitative variable is either discrete or continuous. A discrete variable takes only a countable number of distinct integer values. Examples are the number of members in a family, number of cars in a parking lot, number of mangoes in a tree in an orchard, number of runs scored in a cricket match, etc. A continuous variable can take infinite values in an interval. Examples are speed, distance, time, height, weight, etc. Continuous variables do not take a specific value or an integer value.

Scales of measurements

Scales of measurements depend on the type of data. Qualitative variables are measured using nominal and ordinal measurements. Anything that is named is nominal. When nominal is ordered it becomes ordinal. While the *type* of pizza like vegetarian feast pizza and chicken supreme pizza is nominal, the *size* like small, medium, regular and large, is ordinal. While a shirt is nominal, small, medium, large, extra-large are ordinal. While thyroxin level is nominal, twenty-five mcg, fifty mcg, seventy-five mcg and 100 mcg thyroxin are ordinal. Quantitative variables are measured with ratio and interval scales. The ratio scale of measurement is the scale that is expressible in a ratio a/b (b non-zero) where 'a' and 'b' are two numerical measures. An interval scale is used when the zero is not absolute but used as a reference value. Two fifty-rupee notes make a hundred rupees. A hundred-rupee note and two fifty-rupee notes are the same in value as well as in transaction. Consider water in two kettles named A and B. Water in kettle A is heated to 100 degrees Celsius, and the water in kettle B is heated to fifty degrees Celsius. Now, the temperature of one cup of water from kettle A is not equal to the temperature of two cups of water from kettle B because one is a measure of temperature and the other is a measure of volume. Two fifty-rupee notes make 100 rupees in sum. But two cups of fifty-degree Celsius water do not make 100 degrees Celsius in sum. This is because zero degrees Celsius is not absolute zero but a reference point. Many time-series data are measured from a reference time point, before and after which data points are measured. Care must be taken while handling such data, especially when the data is processed or analysed using software. In simple terms, qualitative data are measured using nominal and ordinal scales, and quantitative data are measured using ratio and interval scales.

Types of data

Data collected is either cross-sectional or time series. Data about one single characteristic or several characteristics at a single time point across different sectors is cross-sectional. The sectors may include individuals, households, firms, industries, regions and countries. A typical cross-sectional data set may look as given below. The data set includes both qualitative like name and occupation, as well as quantitative data like age and annual income.

Case	Name	Age	Annual income in lakhs	Occupation	Gender
1	Raman	45	40	Vice-president	Male
2	Chande	42	35	Senior manager	Male
3	Sheela	37	32	Manager	Female
4	Shilpa	46	42	Vice-president	Female
5	Bindu	34	23	Team leader	Female
6	Vikram	34	35	Consultant	Male
7	Ashwin	32	20	Architect	Male
8	Gopal	34	24	Associate	Male
9	Vijesh	27	18	Analyst	Female
10	Amrita	29	27	Data scientist	Female

The data about one single characteristic or several characteristics over a series of time points in chronological order is a time series. The chronological order may be daily, weekly, bi-weekly, monthly, bi-monthly, yearly or half-yearly. The retail and wholesale price indices, GDP growth rate, consumer price indices, inflation indices, daily, hourly, weekly, annual weather data, daily stock prices, birth rate, death rate, migration rate, global temperature, air quality, etc., are examples of time series data.

Statistics

Statistics is the science that guides extracting information from a data set. A good statistical analysis involves finding the right data, using the appropriate statistical tools, and precisely communicating the extracted information in written language. Statistics is broadly divided into two parts. Descriptive statistics describes the characteristics present in the data. Inferential statistics provides methodologies for extracting information from a sample and generalizing the same to the entire population from where the sample was taken.

Descriptive statistics

Here is a story of a hungry tourist going to a restaurant with only Rs 100 in his pocket. The tourist sees a signboard outside the restaurant: *Today's special: Hot Chicken Burger—Rs 70*. The tourist happily goes inside the restaurant and checks with the waiter if the offer on the signboard is valid. The waiter answers, yes. The tourist orders a chicken burger. After ten minutes, the waiter brings the chicken burger, which is large, hot and smells fresh. After eating the burger, the tourist orders a water bottle for Rs 20. Finally, he pays Rs 100 towards the bill of Rs 90 and tells the waiter to keep Rs 10 as a tip. Now that his hunger is satisfied, the tourist is able to think. He wonders how on earth someone could give such a large chicken burger for just Rs 70. He asks the waiter this question. The waiter replies that they mix horse meat with chicken meat. Again, out of curiosity, the tourist asks the waiter to explain the proportion of horse meat and chicken meat in the mix. The waiter replies fifty-fifty. Still curious, the tourist asks the waiter to explain what he means by fifty-fifty. The waiter coolly replies, 'one horse and one chicken'.

In business scenarios, people frequently use percentages like this.

A popular branded biscuit is named 50-50. People tend to mistake this for salt and sugar in a fifty-fifty ratio. The manufacturing company of this biscuit never claims that the salt and sugar are in a fifty-fifty ratio. In reality, the biscuit just tastes salty and sweet.

Similarly, the government will often make announcements such as they are increasing value added tax (VAT) by 2 per cent from 16 per cent to 18 per cent. This is two percentage points, which is a 12.5 per cent increase. One has to be cautious while making statements based on percentages.

Central tendency

Data collected over a month, or a year, or from hundreds and thousands of people, result in a large set of numbers. It is hard to handle and conclude any valuable information from this large set of numbers. For a quick understanding, usually, a representative number of the data set is used. This is similar to location in the real estate business. In real estate, the location is an important parameter and usually, a township is developed based on location. Similarly, in a data set, the location is important, which is used to represent the entire set of data.

When a bag full of rice is poured on an even surface from a height, the rice forms a heap concentrating at a centre point and spreading on all sides like a mountain. This property is known as central tendency and dispersion. That is, there is a tendency for the data to cluster around a value at the centre. Once the centre is identified as the location, the spread of the rest of the data can be measured with a scale parameter called dispersion. Hence the concepts of location and scale parameters were born. The location is usually measured by the measures of central tendency.

There are three commonly used measures of central tendency, namely, the arithmetic mean, median and mode. These measures are simple to understand. The arithmetic mean is simply the sum of all data points divided by the number of data points. The median divides the data points into two equal portions; the number of data points below and above the median is equal. The mode is the most frequently occurring value in the data points.

The choice of the arithmetic mean, median and mode depends on the data and the purpose of use. While the arithmetic mean is easy to understand and interpret, it is affected by the extreme values present in the data. It is easy to find the median when an odd number of data points are considered. In the case of an even number of data points, the median is not obtainable. In this case, for practical application, the arithmetic mean of the middle two data points is considered the median. The mode is usually not unique. There can be two, three or multiple modes possible for a set of data points. Hence, mode is not preferred for quantitative data. However, the mode is the only measure for qualitative data. For example, food preferences at a get-together, the most-sold medicines in a pharmacy, fast-moving consumer goods in a hypermarket, etc. For quantitative data, the arithmetic mean and median are the two usually used measures of central tendency. While the arithmetic mean is widely used, the median is preferred for data types, salary, income and expenditure. The median salary will indicate where exactly the salary of 50 per cent of the employees lies while the arithmetic mean will under-state or over-state this value. For practical utility, mathematical stability, ease of application and interpretation, the arithmetic mean is widely used.

Is the mean or median better to describe average income? The mean is an average, one of several that summarizes the typical value of a set of data. The median is the middle value in data sorted in ascending or descending order. If the data contains an even number of values, the median is taken as the mean of the middle two. The question as to whether it is better to use the mean or the median may sound like an obscure technical question, but it really can matter. This depends on how the data is distributed. The mean is used with symmetrically distributed data; otherwise, the median is used specially when the data is skewed.

Let X_1, X_2 . . . X_N be N observations pertaining to a variable of interest named X. For example, X can be the height of 100 children. Having a set of N data points in hand it is hard to come to any conclusion or understand the behaviour of the data. It is easy to make sense of and handle if these observations are represented by one single number. That one single number is the average, usually represented by the arithmetic mean. Let the arithmetic mean be denoted by µ to stay in line with universal notations. Then, $\mu = \dfrac{1}{N} \displaystyle\sum_{i=1}^{N} X_i$..

Dispersion

While the set of N observations is represented by one number, µ, it may be of interest to know how scattered the observations in the data set are around this representative number µ. One of the easiest ways of finding the dispersion from the arithmetic mean µ is finding the deviation of all observations from this µ. Thus, the deviations from the arithmetic mean are

$(X_1- \mu, X_2- \mu \ldots X_N- \mu)$. Again, it is easy to make sense and handle if these deviations are represented by one single number similar to that of the arithmetic mean. The arithmetic mean of these deviations is then, $\dfrac{1}{N}\sum\limits_{i-1}^{N}(X_i - \mu)$. When the deviations of data from arithmetic mean are summed, the sum becomes zero. One can easily verify that this becomes zero for any data set. For a quick understanding, consider the data, 2, 4, 3, 6, 5. The arithmetic mean is 20/5 = 4. Now the deviations from the mean are -2, 0, -1, 2, 1. When these deviations are added, the sum is zero. This is natural for any data set. Hence, a theory, *the sum of the deviations from the arithmetic mean is always zero*, was born. As the sum of the deviations is zero, the arithmetic mean of the deviations is also zero. When the arithmetic mean of the deviations is zero, it may be wrongly interpreted that there are no deviations of the data measured from the arithmetic mean. This is known as the zeroing effect. As there are non-zero deviations from the arithmetic mean, to get a proper measure of deviations, this zeroing effect has to be removed. There are two quick solutions to get rid of this zeroing effect and to get an idea about the dispersion of the data from the arithmetic mean. One is squaring the deviations and another is using the absolute values of the deviations.

Consider squaring the deviations. That is, $(X_1- \mu)^2$, $(X_2- \mu)^2 \ldots (X_N- \mu)^2$. The arithmetic mean of these squared deviations is then, $\frac{1}{N}\sum_{i=1}^{N}(X_i - \mu)^2$. A new baby is born, and the baby is named the variance and is denoted by a symbol σ^2. Thus, $\sigma^2 = \frac{1}{N}\sum_{i=1}^{N}(X_i - \mu)^2$. But the interest is to get the arithmetic mean of the deviations. Since the deviations are squared, the unit of the measurement of the variance too gets squared and it becomes difficult to interpret. Hence, the positive square root of the variance $\sigma = \sqrt{\sigma^2} = \sqrt{\frac{1}{N}\sum_{i=1}^{N}(X_i - \mu)^2}$ will give the required measure of the deviations. Again, a new baby is born. This baby is named the standard deviation.

Consider using the absolute deviations. That is, $|X_1 - \mu|$, $|X_2 - \mu|$, . . ., $|X_N - \mu|$. The arithmetic mean of these absolute deviations is then, $\frac{1}{N}\sum_{i=1}^{N}|X_i - \mu|$. The arithmetic mean of absolute deviations when abbreviated becomes MAD. As it reads, one may go mad if this is used on all occasions. For example, the MAD for the data set (-2, -2, -2, -2, 2, 2, 2, 2) is 2.0. Also, the MAD for the data set (-3, -1, -3, -1, 3, 1, 3, 1) is also 2.0. The two data sets have a different dispersion. The second data has a larger dispersion than the first data set. It is easy to understand the wrong representation of dispersion by MAD if used to represent the dispersion in these two sets of data.

The standard deviations for these two data sets are 2.0 and 2.236068 respectively. This simple example shows that the standard deviation is better at representing the dispersion when the data is not uniform. It is not that MAD is not useful. MAD is useful as long as the data behave uniformly. Usually, MAD either underestimates or overestimates the variability in the data. For any data, the standard deviation is more stable. For this reason, the standard deviation is used as a standard measure of dispersion. For obvious reasons, the target is aimed at the average (usually represented by arithmetic mean) and the tolerance is found in multiples of the standard deviation, in the so-called safe zone explained in the previous chapter. Sometimes, the target (average) is called a location parameter and the standard deviation is called a scale parameter.

Data visualization and cleansing

A histogram is a graphical representation of a frequency distribution made up of rectangles whose areas are proportionate to the frequencies. It was invented by Karl Pearson. It is an approximate representation of the numerical data distribution. The class intervals are drawn along the x-axis, and the accompanying frequencies are plotted along the y-axis, to create a histogram. The height of each rectangle is proportional to the frequency of that class, and the width is equal to the class's length. A histogram provides a visual representation of the location, spread and skewness of a data set. It also helps visualize whether the distribution is symmetric, skewed left, skewed right, unimodal, bimodal or multimodal. It shows outliers if any, and gaps in the data.

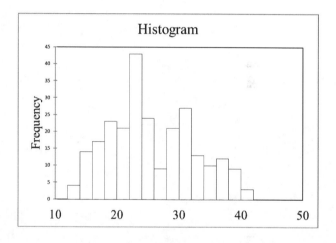

A box plot is a standardized way of displaying the distribution of data based on a five-number summary: the Minimum, the First Quartile (Q1), the Median, the Third Quartile (Q3) and the Maximum. It shows the outliers, if present, in the data. Both histograms and box plots allow for visually assessing the central tendency, the amount of variation in the data as well as the presence of gaps, outliers or unusual data points. Although histograms are better at displaying the distribution of data, a box plot helps to know if the distribution is symmetric or skewed. In a symmetric distribution, the mean and median are nearly the same, and the two whiskers (the distance between the Q1 and Minimum and the distance between the Q3 and the Maximum) have almost the same length.

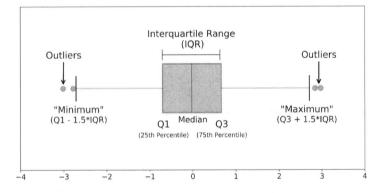

Consider real-life business data related to the production lead time to supply a special type of perishable food. The data given in the table below shows the date of order of the food and the production lead time (in days) to supply the same. The distributor dealing with this product was facing a large number of order cancellations due to his inability to meet the demand on time. Actually the distributor was considering this as one single data set and was working with the wrong safe zone.

OR	PLT	OR	PLT	OR	PLT	OR	PLT	OR	PLT	OR	PLT	OR	PLT	OR	PLT
05-Jan-11	14	15-Feb-11	31	15-Apr-11	30	20-May-11	22	29-Jun-11	23	30-Aug-11	86	04-Oct-11	45	09-Dec-11	21
06-Jan-11	26	18-Feb-11	23	21-Apr-11	13	20-May-11	22	04-Jul-11	18	30-Aug-11	89	04-Oct-11	59	09-Dec-11	35
07-Jan-11	25	18-Feb-11	27	21-Apr-11	57	20-May-11	25	04-Jul-11	82	30-Aug-11	103	06-Oct-11	29	12-Dec-11	18
07-Jan-11	27	18-Feb-11	27	26-Apr-11	20	23-May-11	25	05-Jul-11	17	30-Aug-11	114	07-Oct-11	21	13-Dec-11	15
07-Jan-11	30	18-Feb-11	36	26-Apr-11	24	25-May-11	17	11-Jul-11	16	02-Sep-11	28	13-Oct-11	22	13-Dec-11	22
07-Jan-11	30	22-Feb-11	23	28-Apr-11	34	25-May-11	23	13-Jul-11	13	02-Sep-11	28	14-Oct-11	32	13-Dec-11	29
11-Jan-11	23	24-Feb-11	58	29-Apr-11	16	25-May-11	23	13-Jul-11	17	06-Sep-11	17	20-Oct-11	29	13-Dec-11	32
11-Jan-11	23	01-Mar-11	22	02-May-11	13	25-May-11	23	13-Jul-11	24	06-Sep-11	36	20-Oct-11	35	13-Dec-11	39
11-Jan-11	23	02-Mar-11	20	02-May-11	14	25-May-11	25	13-Jul-11	27	07-Sep-11	73	20-Oct-11	38	15-Dec-11	28
12-Jan-11	20	02-Mar-11	21	02-May-11	18	26-May-11	30	14-Jul-11	22	08-Sep-11	34	20-Oct-11	42	15-Dec-11	34
12-Jan-11	20	02-Mar-11	22	02-May-11	52	26-May-11	32	14-Jul-11	22	12-Sep-11	18	31-Oct-11	25	15-Dec-11	36
14-Jan-11	23	02-Mar-11	22	03-May-11	10	26-May-11	33	19-Jul-11	19	12-Sep-11	40	02-Nov-11	17	15-Dec-11	36
14-Jan-11	23	02-Mar-11	25	03-May-11	17	26-May-11	33	21-Jul-11	65	14-Sep-11	30	03-Nov-11	21	15-Dec-11	45
14-Jan-11	43	02-Mar-11	31	05-May-11	18	26-May-11	40	25-Jul-11	18	14-Sep-11	30	03-Nov-11	22	16-Dec-11	28
14-Jan-11	43	09-Mar-11	42	05-May-11	18	26-May-11	41	25-Jul-11	18	14-Sep-11	72	03-Nov-11	31	16-Dec-11	28
14-Jan-11	53	21-Mar-11	17	06-May-11	62	27-May-11	23	25-Jul-11	19	15-Sep-11	56	03-Nov-11	31	16-Dec-11	36
14-Jan-11	58	21-Mar-11	20	09-May-11	33	31-May-11	21	25-Jul-11	22	19-Sep-11	25	04-Nov-11	21	16-Dec-11	36

24-Jan-11	23	22-Mar-11	16	13-May-11	15	01-Jun-11	25	25-Jul-11	27	19-Sep-11	25	14-Nov-11	18	16-Dec-11	49
24-Jan-11	30	22-Mar-11	19	13-May-11	22	01-Jun-11	60	25-Jul-11	29	19-Sep-11	32	14-Nov-11	22	19-Dec-11	45
25-Jan-11	22	23-Mar-11	14	13-May-11	22	08-Jun-11	15	25-Jul-11	36	19-Sep-11	39	14-Nov-11	25	19-Dec-11	45
25-Jan-11	22	23-Mar-11	14	17-May-11	28	08-Jun-11	28	25-Jul-11	36	19-Sep-11	81	14-Nov-11	27	19-Dec-11	52
28-Jan-11	44	25-Mar-11	38	17-May-11	31	08-Jun-11	28	26-Jul-11	18	20-Sep-11	15	14-Nov-11	30	19-Dec-11	58
28-Jan-11	44	28-Mar-11	16	17-May-11	31	08-Jun-11	29	26-Jul-11	21	21-Sep-11	25	14-Nov-11	32	19-Dec-11	60
01-Feb-11	22	29-Mar-11	15	17-May-11	34	09-Jun-11	17	26-Jul-11	29	21-Sep-11	30	14-Nov-11	37	19-Dec-11	60
01-Feb-11	22	29-Mar-11	25	17-May-11	35	09-Jun-11	56	27-Jul-11	23	21-Sep-11	30	14-Nov-11	38	19-Dec-11	60
03-Feb-11	35	31-Mar-11	18	17-May-11	35	10-Jun-11	24	27-Jul-11	70	21-Sep-11	30	14-Nov-11	38	19-Dec-11	66
04-Feb-11	19	31-Mar-11	32	18-May-11	30	13-Jun-11	25	01-Aug-11	20	21-Sep-11	39	16-Nov-11	25	19-Dec-11	66
04-Feb-11	33	04-Apr-11	16	18-May-11	73	22-Jun-11	21	04-Aug-11	22	21-Sep-11	52	16-Nov-11	31	19-Dec-11	66
08-Feb-11	15	04-Apr-11	19	18-May-11	74	22-Jun-11	21	04-Aug-11	22	21-Sep-11	52	21-Nov-11	32	19-Dec-11	67
08-Feb-11	15	04-Apr-11	25	19-May-11	14	22-Jun-11	22	08-Aug-11	18	21-Sep-11	58	22-Nov-11	17	19-Dec-11	67
08-Feb-11	15	04-Apr-11	28	19-May-11	23	22-Jun-11	23	09-Aug-11	38	21-Sep-11	60	22-Nov-11	31	19-Dec-11	67
08-Feb-11	18	06-Apr-11	14	19-May-11	23	22-Jun-11	28	10-Aug-11	16	21-Sep-11	60	23-Nov-11	30	19-Dec-11	67
08-Feb-11	21	08-Apr-11	56	19-May-11	25	22-Jun-11	28	10-Aug-11	20	22-Sep-11	29	29-Nov-11	17	19-Dec-11	68
08-Feb-11	22	08-Apr-11	56	19-May-11	26	22-Jun-11	28	10-Aug-11	21	22-Sep-11	30	29-Nov-11	23	19-Dec-11	68

08-Feb-11	28	08-Apr-11	56	19-May-11	34	23-Jun-11	22	10-Aug-11	51	22-Sep-11	30	29-Nov-11	23	21-Dec-11	24
08-Feb-11	36	15-Apr-11	19	19-May-11	47	24-Jun-11	21	10-Aug-11	81	27-Sep-11	24	02-Dec-11	19	21-Dec-11	24
08-Feb-11	64	15-Apr-11	19	19-May-11	48	27-Jun-11	12	12-Aug-11	21	27-Sep-11	39	02-Dec-11	27	22-Dec-11	29
11-Feb-11	73	15-Apr-11	19	19-May-11	70	27-Jun-11	18	16-Aug-11	24	27-Sep-11	46	02-Dec-11	30	22-Dec-11	43
14-Feb-11	32	15-Apr-11	30	19-May-11	72	28-Jun-11	16	30-Aug-11	31	29-Sep-11	32	06-Dec-11	24	29-Dec-11	37
15-Feb-11	22	15-Apr-11	30	19-May-11	73	28-Jun-11	122	30-Aug-11	36	04-Oct-11	40	09-Dec-11	21	29-Dec-11	50

OR: Order Date. PLT: Production Lead Time

The histogram of the probability distribution of the production lead time is depicted in the figure below.

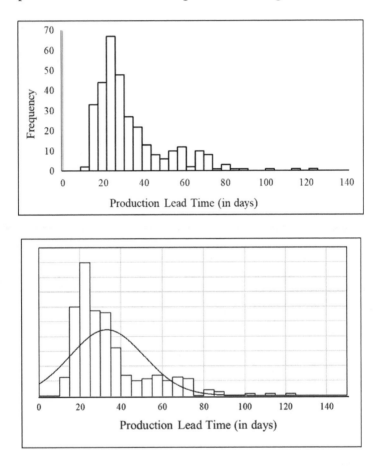

One can see that the data is heavily skewed to the right from the centre. The original data set, if broken into two parts A and B as shown in the figure given below can better explain the behaviour of the production lead time. Breaking the project lead time data into two parts makes sense in interpreting the results. Projections based on the two means with two parts of the data will provide the best results and cancellation of orders may be minimized. The distributer has to work with two average production lead times and agree to supply accordingly.

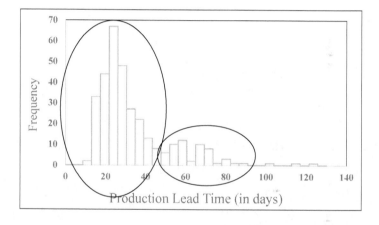

Interestingly, it can be seen from the above figure that the two parts A and B look almost symmetric but not perfectly symmetric. The nature of the distribution of the data belonging to parts A and B can be understood with the help of box plots. The box plots for the two data parts are presented below.

The box plot of the portion 'A' of the histogram shows that the distribution is almost symmetrical but slightly right-skewed. This skew-ness can be practically managed by the distributor.

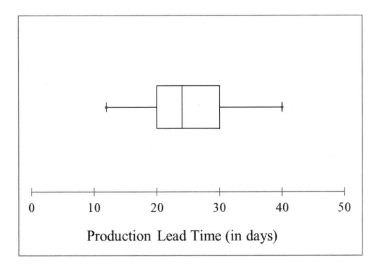

The box plot of the portion 'B' of the histogram shows the distribution is symmetric but has few outliers.

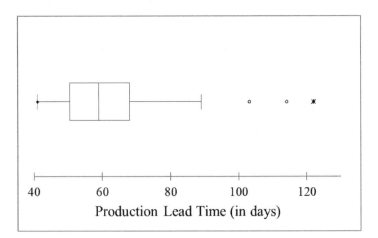

The data is well defined until the production lead time is eighty days. Beyond eighty days the data is skewed. There are outliers seen in the box plot. These outliers must be discarded from the data. The distributer shall have to avoid suppliers beyond eighty days to avoid the cancellation of orders.

A relative measure of dispersion

The standard deviation serves as a measure to understand the extent of variability in a data set measured from the mean. Depending on the magnitude of data points, a higher numerical value of the standard deviation means higher variability in the data and vice versa. This is also used to compare the variability in several variables. However, a little caution is taken when comparing variables measured in different units of measurements similar to comparing oranges with apples. For such a comparison, a relative measure is used. The simple relative measure is the standard deviation divided by the arithmetic mean and expressed in percentage. This new baby is termed the coefficient of variation. The coefficient of variation is a ratio and is usually expressed in percentages. The higher this value for any variable, the more the variability of the data about that variable. This helps in the easy comparison of several variables with different units of measurement.

Relationships in data—correlation and regression

Let two variables, say X and Y are studied together. Suppose the interest is to know if there exists any relationship between these two variables. It is necessary to know the averages and the dispersions of these two variables to understand the simultaneous variation in the two variables. Let $X_1, X_2, \ldots, X_N$ and $Y_1, Y_2, \ldots, Y_N$ be the observations on X and Y respectively. Let μ_X and μ_Y be the arithmetic means of X and Y. The deviations of the observations on X and Y from their respective means are $(X_1 - \mu_X, X_2 - \mu_X, \ldots, X_N - \mu_X)$ and $(Y_1 - \mu_Y, Y_2 - \mu_Y, \ldots, Y_N - \mu_Y)$. The simultaneous deviations are the product of these deviations, $(X - \mu_X)(Y - \mu_Y)$. There will be as many products of the deviations as the number of pairs of observations and therefore be represented by the arithmetic mean of the products of the deviations. That is, $\dfrac{1}{N} \sum_{i}^{N} (X_i - \mu_X)(Y_i - \mu_Y)$. This new baby is named the covariance between X and Y. This covariance can be negative or positive. The negative sign indicates that these variables move in opposite directions. That is, if one variable increases (or decreases), then the other decreases (or increases). The positive sign indicates that these variables move in the same direction. That is, if one variable increases (or decreases), then the other variable increases (or decreases). If the covariance is zero or close to zero, it may be concluded that there is no influence of one variable on the other.

The covariance shows the variability of the two variables, which also includes the individual variability of the two variables concerned. When the individual variabilities are removed from this covariance, only the relationship, if any, between the two variables remains in the covariance. Hence it can be seen that

$$\frac{\frac{1}{N} \sum_{i=1}^{N} (X_i - \mu_X)(Y_i - \mu_Y)}{SD(X) \cdot SD(Y)}$$ gives only the relationship.

This new baby is termed the correlation coefficient, denoted by 'r'. The absolute value of this ratio can at the maximum be equal to 1. Depending upon whether the covariance is negative or positive, this ratio is also positive or negative. Hence, the correlation coefficient lies between -1 and +1. It is common sense to understand that the correlation can be considered significant whenever the ratio is closer to either -1 or +1. When this correlation coefficient is zero or close to zero, it implies that no relationship is exhibited in the data on the two variables concerned. The squared value of the correlation coefficient (r^2), which is called the coefficient of determination, measures the amount of variability in Y explained by the X and vice versa and is usually expressed in percentage.

The covariance between the two variables X and Y is the arithmetic mean of the products of the deviations from their respective means. As covariance is a means to find if the two variables are related, the increase or decrease of one variable may result in an increase or decrease in the other variable. This is known as the cause-and-effect relationship. In the covariance, if the variance of one variable is silenced, the covariance may then contain the relationship and the variability of the other variable. That is the influence of one variable on the other variable in terms of variance. This results in two possible expressions, namely, $\dfrac{\frac{1}{N}\sum_{i=1}^{N}\left(X_i - \mu_X\right)\left(Y_i - \mu_Y\right)}{V(X)}$ and $\dfrac{\frac{1}{N}\sum_{i=1}^{N}\left(X_i - \mu_X\right)\left(Y_i - \mu_Y\right)}{V(Y)}$. The first expression will have the variability of Y in the covariance term and the second expression will have the variability of X in the covariance term. The first expression gives the rate of change of Y with respect to X and the second expression gives the rate of change of X with respect to Y. These two new expressions respectively are termed regression coefficients of Y on X, denoted by b_{yx} and X on Y, denoted by b_{xy}. The covariance term in the regression coefficient of Y on X expression contains the variance of Y induced by X, known as explained variance, and due to other factors not taken into account is known as unexplained variance and vice versa. If the relationship between the variables is linear, the relationship is usually represented by the equation of a straight line, $y = a + b_{yx}(x)$, where y and x represent values of X and Y, a is the intercept and b_{yx} is the regression coefficient of Y on X. Similarly, the regression equation of X on Y can be written as $y = a + b_{xy}(x)$ where b_{xy} is the regression coefficient of X on Y.

The squared value of the correlation coefficient (R^2) is known as the coefficient of determination and is usually expressed in percentages by simply multiplying by 100. When used along with regression, the coefficient of determination explains how much variation in one variable (usually the dependent variable) is explained by the other variable (usually the independent variable). In regression, the dependent variable is known as the response variable and the independent variable is known as the explanatory variable or the predictor. The linear relationship between one response variable and one explanatory variable is called the linear regression between two variables. The linear relationship between one response variable and two or more explanatory variables is called multiple linear regression. In practice, the relationship among variables need not be linear.

Nature of relationships

The natural relationship between two variables can be positive where an increase or decrease in one variable results in an increase or decrease in another variable. That is, both variables move in the same direction. The relationship can be negative where an increase or decrease in one variable results in a decrease or an increase in another variable. That is, the variables move in opposite directions. There may not exist any relationship between the two variables that are being studied. These three types of scenarios are explained in the figure below.

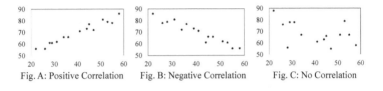

Fig. A: Positive Correlation   Fig. B: Negative Correlation   Fig. C: No Correlation

The age, height and weight of humans are closely related. As one's age increases, one's height also increases until a certain age, and as one's height increases, one's weight also increases. Thus, age, height and weight exhibit positive relationships. While the correlation brings out whether age, height and weight are related, the regression brings out the cause-and-effect relationship among them. For example, if a person's age is forty years, then what is the weight of the person? If a person's height is 170 centimetres, then what is their weight in kilograms? These relationships are also useful in calculating the body mass index (BMI), which is used to assess whether a person is obese or overweight or normal.

Example—students in an MBA programme

The following is an example of real data collected from a class of sixty students. Using this data set, the analyses and interpretation using descriptive measures explained in this section are illustrated.

The data on age (in years), height (in centimetres) and weight (in kilograms) of sixty-three students enrolled in an MBA programme are furnished in the table below.

Age	Height	Weight	Age	Height	Weight	Age	Height	Weight
25	187	83	28	167	70	27	159	51
25	182	87	28	170	80	27	187	80
25	162	58	28	178	76	31	177	69
25	170	69	29	165	50	27	155	61
25	185	79	29	166	60	29	176	76
26	172	74	30	172	65	27	187	86
26	153	55	30	157	60	26	175	60
26	165	74	30	160	56	27	177	81
26	175	62	31	155	51	27	160	67
26	153	51	30	183	83	28	180	75
26	170	62	32	172	70	28	173	76
26	166	70	27	165	67	26	166	72
27	180	87	27	163	72	28	173	56
27	176	85	26	168	73	25	175	73
27	180	87	27	170	70	27	160	50
27	156	73	26	175	68	27	167	75
27	172	64	27	173	70	28	165	68
27	174	63	28	168	79	33	170	78
27	165	75	29	174	71	28	154	62
28	173	84	28	160	65	31	180	78
28	180	80	26	164	55	31	160	60

The students were selected from all over India following a well-defined admission criterion. This is a typical data set that one may observe in practical situations when data on characteristics are obtained at a given point of time in a region. This is also known as the natural phenomenon that which the data are not influenced by external factors. In most business situations this is the case. Sometimes, data affected by known or unknown, or by both known and unknown factors are also present in real-life situations. Careful data visualization efforts will reduce possible wrong inferences about the characteristics inferred from the data.

The data descriptives are given in the following table.

Age		Height		Weight	
Mean	27.54	Mean	169.79	Mean	69.63
Median	27	Median	170	Median	70
Mode	27	Mode	170	Mode	70
Range	7	Range	34	Range	37
Minimum	25	Minimum	153	Minimum	50
Maximum	32	Maximum	187	Maximum	87
Standard deviation	1.748	Standard deviation	8.783	Standard deviation	10.108
Coefficient of variation	6.348	Coefficient of variation	5.173	Coefficient of variation	14.515

From the descriptive statistics, it may be observed that the mean, median and mode are almost the same in all three variables of age, height and weight considered in the study. This indicates that the data exhibit a symmetric distribution. In addition, mean ± 3S.D includes all data values in age, height and weight. This is a case of normal distribution known as the bell curve.

The coefficient of variation helps understand which variable varies more when a set of variables measured in different units of measurement are considered. In the example, the coefficient of variation of age = 6.348%, height = 5.17277% and weight = 14.5157%. The students of this MBA programme vary more in weight compared to age and height, vary more in age compared to height, and all the students vary least in height.

The correlation among the three variables age, height and weight considered here are,

	Age	Height
Age	1	
Height	-0.081	1
Weigh	-0.081	0.71495

It is observed that height and weight show a significant linear correlation whereas age has almost no correlation with height or weight. Hence it is natural to study the cause-and-effect relationship between height and weight using linear regression. As in reality, weight is influenced by height, a linear regression equation of weight as a function of height is found using the given data. The results are,

Weight = -73.6207 + 0.844877(Height)

with an R^2=52.15%. That is, about 53 per cent of the variation in weight is explained by height. A high negative intercept value shows that weight is also influenced by another variable or other variables, which need to be studied. This is how one can explore relationships from data. The below figure explains the linear regression between weight and height. The spread of the data points around the straight line shows the variability of weight around height. The closer the points are to the straight line the better the regression.

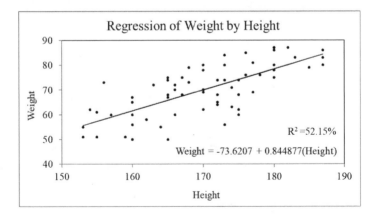

Another important concept in regression is the residual. Let X (independent) and Y (dependent) be the two variables considered. The regression equation between Y and X is Y = a + bX. Given data, the values of 'a' and 'b' are obtained. In the example, Y is weight and X is height. The regression equation is Y = -73.6207 + 0.844877X. Using this equation, for given values of X, the estimates of Y can be obtained. These estimates are known as $\widehat{Y}$. The difference, Y-$\widehat{Y}$ is the residual. Residual is the portion of Y not explained by the regression. A plot of the residual values explains how good the regression is. A closer spread of residuals about zero is usually desired, because the estimates $\widehat{Y}$ of Y provided by the regression equation result in the residuals (Y-$\widehat{Y}$). In this situation, the regression is said to be good and explains the response variable well.

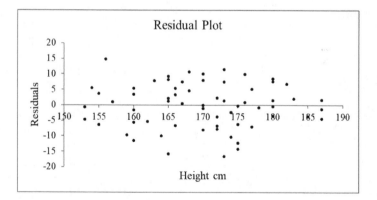

The above figure explains the residual plot of weight on height. The spread is around zero, well spread without showing any pattern. This indicates the relationship between weight and height can be linear, and weight can be explained by height. However, a larger spread around zero also explains the possible involvement of another or other variables.

3

Probability and Probability Distributions

What is random?

To understand probability, a clear understanding of the term 'random' is necessary. What is random? Random is something unique for everyone to appreciate only by its feel. Suppose someone is driving a car and comes upon an intersection. The traffic at the intersection is managed by a traffic policeman. The driver of the car has three choices—he can turn left, turn right or go straight through. The driver knows in which direction he will go as he knows his destination. The traffic policeman knows all three possible directions the driver can take but does not know the actual direction the driver will take until the driver turns on the car's indicator. The direction the driver takes is random to the policeman.

In a hypermarket, a customer has four choices of payment, namely, cash, coupon, credit card or debit card. Both the cashier and the customer know all these four permissible payment modes in advance. While the customer knows the mode of payment in advance (as he/she is the payer), the cashier will have no clue about the same until the customer makes the payment. The mode of payment by the customer is random for the cashier.

Let us consider how one purchases a car. A budget is decided. Within the budget, one identifies the available makes and models. Suppose one narrows down the choice to five makes. Say that each make has five models—sedan, hatchback, SUV, sports and convertible. Each of these models has three fuel types (petrol, diesel and electric), two transmission system options (manual and auto) and seven colour variants. Ignoring the seating type and room space, it can be seen that there are $5 \times 5 \times 3 \times 2 \times 7 = 1050$ options available for the purchase of a new car. Though all these 1050 options are known in advance, the car finally purchased is not known until the purchase is made.

A family goes to a restaurant for dinner. The waiter offers them a menu. There are about a hundred food choices available on the menu card. The family finally orders their choice of food. The chef in the kitchen knows in advance all the possible food choices (printed on the menu card) the family may order but does not know the actual food ordered until the order reaches the chef. The food the family orders is random for the chef.

The duration of a call received on a mobile phone is random. The duration is certainly more than zero seconds and can take any value, which is known when the call ends. The duration of the call is random.

Random experiment and sample space

A random experiment is an experiment in which all possible outcomes are known in advance, but the outcome of a particular trial is unknown until the trial is completed. The possible outcomes of a random experiment constitute a sample space represented by a set denoted by S.

| Random Experiment | $\implies$ | All Possible Outcomes | $\implies$ | Sample Space |

Discrete sample space

A sample space is discrete if the elements in the sample space can be counted, such as 1, 2, 3, etc. For example, in a single roll of a die, the sample space is, $S = (1, 2, 3, 4, 5, 6)$ and for a roll of two dice together, the sample space is $S = \{(1,1), (1,2), (1,3), (1,4), (1,5), (1,6), (2,1), (2,2), (2,3), (2,4), (2,5), (2,6), (3,1), (3,2), (3,3), (3,4), (3,5), (3,6), (4,1), (4,2), (4,3), (4,4), (4,5), (4,6), (5,1), (5,2), (5,3), (5,4), (5,5), (5,6), (6,1), (6,2), (6,3), (6,4), (6,5), (6,6)\}$.

If an experiment is described as a sequence of k steps with n_1 possible outcomes in the first step, n_2 possible outcomes in the second step, and so on, n_k

possible outcomes in the kth step, then the total number of outcomes would be $n_1 \times n_2 \times n_3 \times \cdots \times n_k$. For example, consider an organization that has five home bases and employs a staff comprising two genders, spread across twenty job classifications, and with six education levels. There are 5x2x20x6 = 1200 possible combinations of the employees and hence the sample space of a randomly chosen employee will contain 1200 elements. It is practically not possible to represent them in a set and hence for an understanding they are mathematically enumerated.

A new software development project has two sequential stages, architecture, and coding and testing. An analysis of past projects reveals 2, 3 or 4 months of possible completion times for the architecture stage and 6, 7 or 8 months of possible completion times for the coding and testing stage. The set of possible completion times of the project can be visualized using a tree diagram.

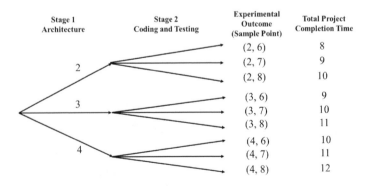

Stage 1 Architecture	Stage 2 Coding and Testing	Experimental Outcome (Sample Point)	Total Project Completion Time
		(2, 6)	8
2		(2, 7)	9
		(2, 8)	10
		(3, 6)	9
3		(3, 7)	10
		(3, 8)	11
		(4, 6)	10
4		(4, 7)	11
		(4, 8)	12

The last column in the above table provides the total project completion time, which is the sample space for the project completion time with combinations of architecture and the coding and testing stages. If the client expects the entire project to be completed in ten months, then it can be seen from the tree diagram that there are six outcomes satisfying the required timeline. Complicated real-life business decisions can be made simple with the help of a tree diagram.

Sometimes combinatorial mathematics is also used to find the sample space. The number of ways n objects can be selected from a set of N objects is given by the combination $^{N}C_{n} = \dfrac{N!}{n!(N-n)!}$, where N! = N(N - 1)(N - 2) . . . (2)(1), n!=n(n-1)(n-2) . . . (2)(1) and 0!=1. The number of ways n objects can be selected from a set of N objects, where the order of selection is important is given by the permutation $^{N}P_{n} = \dfrac{N!}{(N-n)!}$.

Continuous sample space

The sample space is said to be continuous if it is described by an interval. For instance, the sample space for the duration of a randomly selected cell phone call is, S={X | X > 0}. Similarly, S={X | 0 < X < 5} describes the sample space for the GPA of a randomly chosen student.

Events

In most practical cases, the outcomes in a sample space are used to define a happening. The happening is called an event. An element, or a combination of elements, in a sample space constitute an event. An event is simply a subset in the sample space. A simple event, or an elementary event, is a single element (outcome) in the sample space.

Consider the random experiment of tossing a balanced coin. The sample space for this experiment is S={H, T}, where H stands for heads and T stands for tails. Observing a head or a tail is a simple event. As the coin is assumed to be a balanced coin, the chance of observing the event a head or the event a tail is fifty-fifty and hence both are equally likely. Similarly, the sample space for the results of a lottery is S = {win, lose}. Are the events 'win' or 'lose' equally likely? Though 'win' or 'lose' appear similar events to the two events 'head' or 'tail' in tossing a coin once, these events 'win' or 'lose' are not equally likely. This is because in a lottery scheme only one ticket can win and the remaining tickets lose.

A compound event is made up of two or more simple events combined. Many different compound events are usually feasible for a sample space. A rule can be used to describe compound events. The compound event of rolling a seven on a two-dice roll, for example, is made up of six simple events: S=(1,6), (2,5), (3,4), (4,3), (5,2), (6,1).

Probability

It is interesting to discover the possibilities of the occurrence of events based on the results of a random experiment and the events defined in the sample space. The *probability* of an occurrence is a number that expresses the possibility that it will occur. The probability of event 'A' lies within the interval [0, 1]. That is $0 \leq P(A) \leq 1$. If $P(A)=0$, then the event cannot occur. If $P(A)=1$, then the event will certainly occur. It is important to know that probability is not defined but *associated* with every outcome of a random experiment defined in a sample space.

Customers who purchase products online from Amazon pay through one of the four modes of payment, namely, credit card, debit card, cash on delivery and coupons. It is observed that 40 per cent of the customers pay by credit card, 25 per cent of the customers pay by debit card, 20 per cent of the customers pay cash on delivery and 15 per cent of the customers pay by coupons. This information leads to the assignment of the probabilities P(credit card)=0.40, P(debit card)=0.25, P(cash on delivery)=0.20, and P(coupons)=0.15. This is an example of assigning probabilities in a discrete sample space. If the sample space is discrete the probabilities of all events add up to 1. That is, $P(S)=P(E_1)+P(E_2)+ \ldots +P(E_n)=1$ where, $E_1, E_2, \ldots, E_n$ are the events defined in the sample space $S=(E_1, E_2, \ldots, E_n)$.

Approaches to assigning probabilities

There are three approaches to assigning probability, namely, classical approach, relative frequency or empirical approach, and subjective approach. The classical approach is used when the events are equally likely. There is a 50 per cent chance of getting heads on a coin flip (P(Head) = P(Tail) = 0.5).

The relative frequency or empirical approach is used for events based on experimentation or historical data. There is a 3 per cent chance of defective products in a randomly chosen sample from a batch of products. This is the so-called textbook definition of probability—the favourable number of cases divided by the total number of cases.

A subjective approach is used based on the assignor's (subjective) judgment. The probability of precipitation is a subjective probability based on past observations combined with current weather conditions.

A probability is always interpreted in the relative frequency approach no matter which method is used to assign probabilities. In the example of the new software development project, the sample space for the completion time of the project is S = {(2,6), (2,7), (2,8), (3,6), (3,7), (3,8), (4,6), (4,7), (4,8)}. From the sample space, it is found that the possible duration for the completion of the project is eight, nine, ten, eleven and twelve months. The probability of completing the project in exactly eight months is 1/9. The probability of completing the project in ten months is 6/9 (completing the project in ten months means completing the project exactly in 8 or 9 or 10 months).

Types of probability

There are several types of combinations and relationships between or among events. Complement event of event A, denoted by A^c is an event consisting of all the sample points other than A. This means that $P(A)+P(A^c)=1$. The intersection of events A and B is the set of all the sample points that are in both A and B. The joint probability of A and B is the probability of the intersection of A and B and is denoted as $P(A \cap B)$. The union of two events A and B is the event containing all the sample points that are in A or B or both. The union of A and B is denoted as AUB or A or B. Two events are mutually exclusive if they cannot occur together. When two events are mutually exclusive their joint probability is 0. Mutually exclusive means no points in common.

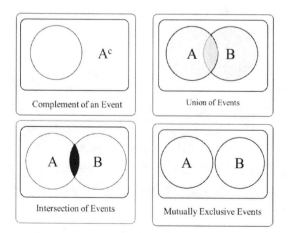

Complement of an Event

Union of Events

Intersection of Events

Mutually Exclusive Events

Joint and marginal probabilities

Operations such as the complement, the union and the intersection of events lead to the concepts of marginal and joint probabilities. These concepts can be better understood through an example.

A fruit jam manufacturer buys mangoes in bulk from a few orchards. Some of the orchards have only grafted varieties of mangoes and some have only non-grafted varieties of mangoes. Grafted varieties are usually juicier and sweeter than non-grafted varieties. The following table compares a sample of 300 mangoes from orchards with grafted varieties and orchards with non-grafted varieties of mangoes.

	Juicy and sweet	Not juicy and sweet
Orchards with grafted varieties of mangoes	90	45
Orchards with non-grafted varieties of mangoes	60	105

The above data is an example of a random experiment where a mango randomly taken from the 300 mangoes can be juicy and sweet, not juicy and sweet, from orchards with grafted varieties of mangoes and from orchards with non-grafted varieties of mangoes. These are the four simple events. For ease of understanding, the following short names are used:

O_1 = Orchards with grafted varieties of mangoes
O_2 = Orchards with non-grafted varieties of mangoes
J_1 = Juicy and sweet
J_2 = Not juicy and sweet

The data now is presented simply:

	J_1	J_2
O_1	90	45
O_2	60	105

The cell frequencies in the above table are the joint occurrence of these events. For example, the cell frequency 90 is the event that the mangoes are from the orchard with grafted varieties and are juicy and sweet.

The cell frequencies in the table represent the joint occurrence of the events. The probability of their joint occurrence is known as the joint probability. These probabilities are computed using the total possible outcomes.

	J_1	J_2	Total
O_1	90	45	135
O_2	60	105	165
Total	150	150	300

	J_1	J_2	Total
O_1	90/300 = 0.30	45/300 = 0.15	135/300 = 0.45
O_2	60/300 = 0.20	105/300 = 0.35	165/300 = 0.55
Total	150/300 = 0.50	150/300 = 0.50	1.00

The joint probabilities are the probabilities of the cells. For example, the joint probability that the mango is juicy and sweet and is from the orchard with grafted varieties of mangoes is 0.30. That is, $P(O_1 \cap J_1) = 0.30$. The joint probability that the mango is juicy and sweet and is from the orchard with non-grafted varieties of mangoes is 0.20. That is, $P(O_2 \cap J_1) = 0.20$. The joint probability that the mango is not juicy and sweet and is from the orchard with grafted varieties of mangoes is 0.15. That is $P(O_1 \cap J_2) = 0.15$. The joint probability that the mango is not juicy and sweet and is from the orchard with non-grafted varieties of mangoes is 0.35. That is $P(O_2 \cap J_2) = 0.50$.

The row totals and column totals represent the occurrence of the simple events, orchards with grafted varieties of mangoes, orchards with non-grafted varieties of mangoes, juicy and sweet and not juicy and sweet. The probabilities of these simple events are the marginal probabilities. Marginal probabilities are found by adding across rows and adding down the columns. The probability that the mango is from the orchard with grafted varieties of mangoes is 0.45. That is, $P(O_1) = 0.45$. The probability that the mango is juicy and sweet, $P(J_1) = 0.50$. The probability that the mango is from the orchard with non-grafted varieties of mangoes is 0.55. That is, $P(O_2) = 0.55$. The probability that the mango is not juicy and sweet, $P(J_2) = 0.50$. The sum of the marginal probabilities is equal to 1. That is $P(O_1) + P(O_2) = 0.45 + 0.55 = 1.0$ and $P(J_1) + P(J_2) = 0.50 + 0.50 = 1.0$.

Conditional probability

Consider a mango chosen randomly from a sample of 300. The probability that the mango is juicy and sweet is $P(J_1) = 0.50$. This is the marginal probability that the mango is juicy and sweet. Supposing the additional information that the chosen mango is from an orchard with grafted varieties of mangoes is given, then the probability that the mango is juicy and sweet will be 90/135 or $0.30/0.45 = 2/3 \approx 0.67$. This is known as the conditional probability given an event. The probability that the mango is juicy and sweet given that it is from the orchard with grafted varieties of mangoes is a conditional probability. That is, $P(J_1|O_1) = 0.67$. See the change in the probability when conditioned on another event. The marginal probability $P(J_1) = 0.50$ has become $P(J_1|O_1) = 0.67$.

Marginal probabilities are known as prior probabilities or priory, and conditional probabilities are known as posterior probabilities. This understanding leads to a relation that $P(J_1|O_1) = 0.30/0.45 = P(J_1 \cap O_1)/P(O_1) \approx 0.67$. Similarly, the conditional probability that the mango is juicy and sweet given that it is from the orchard with non-grafted varieties of mangoes is $P(J_1|O_2) = P(J_1 \cap O_2)/P(O_1) = 0.20/0.55 \approx 0.36$. The conditional probability that the mango is not juicy and sweet given that it is from the orchard with grafted varieties of mangoes is $P(J_2|O_1) = P(J_2 \cap O_1)/P(O_1)$ $0.15/0.45 \approx 0.33$ and the conditional probability that the mango is juicy and sweet given that it is from the orchard with non-grafted varieties of mangoes is $P(J_2|O_2) = P(J_2 \cap O_2)/P(O_2) = 0.35/0.55 \approx 0.64$.

Product rule of probability

The probability of occurrence of an event given that another event has already occurred is the conditional probability. Let M and N be two events.

The conditional probability, $P(M|N) = \dfrac{P(M \text{ and } N)}{P(N)} = \dfrac{P(M \cap N)}{P(N)}$.

The conditional probability $P(N|M) = \dfrac{P(N \text{ and } M)}{P(M)} = \dfrac{P(M \cap N)}{P(M)}$.

$$P(M|N) = \dfrac{P(M \text{ and } N)}{P(N)} = \dfrac{P(M \cap N)}{P(N)}$$

$$P(N|M) = \dfrac{P(N \text{ and } M)}{P(M)} = \dfrac{P(M \cap N)}{P(M)}$$

The above two expressions of conditional probabilities result in the product rule,

$P(M \text{ and } N) = P(M \cap N) = P(M|N)P(N) = P(N|M)P(M).$

Independent events

The joint probability of any two events is the product of conditional probability and marginal probability. This result is used to check whether two events are independent or dependent. The two events M and N can be independent if their joint probability is equal to the product of their marginal probabilities. That is, $P(M$ and $N) = P(M \cap N) = P(M) \bullet P(N)$. This means $P(M|N) = P(M)$. Verbally stated, the conditional probability of an event given another event is the marginal probability of the event.

In the example, the marginal probability that the mango is juicy and sweet is $P(J_1) = 0.5$. The conditional probability that the mango is juicy and sweet, given that it is taken from the orchard with grafted varieties of mangoes, is $P(J_1|O_1) = P(J_1$ and $O_1)/P(O_1) = P(J_1 \cap O_1)/P(O_1) = 0.30/0.45 \approx 0.67$. Here $P(J_1|O_1) = 0.67 \neq P(J_1) = 0.5$. As $P(J_1|O_1) \neq P(J_1)$, the events J_1 and O_1 are not independent.

Addition rule

The union of two events M and N is the occurrence of M or N. Consider the union of two events in the mango example. Consider the probability that a randomly selected mango is juicy and sweet or from an orchard with grafted varieties of mangoes. That is, $P(J_1$ or $O_1)$. The event J_1 or O_1 occurs, whenever J_1 and O_1 occur, J_1 and O_2 occur or J_2 and O_1 occur.

J_1 and O_1 occur J_1 and O_2 occur J_2 and O_1 occur

	J_1	J_2	$P(O_i)$
O_1	0.30	0.15	0.45
O_2	0.20	0.35	0.55
$P(J_i)$	0.50	0.50	1.00

$$P(J_1 \text{ or } O_1) = P(J_1 \cap O_1) + P(J_1 \cap O_2) + P(J_2 \cap O_1) =$$
$$0.30 + 0.20 + 0.15 = 0.65$$

Alternatively, this probability can be computed using the complement probability. The probability of J_1 or O_1 is the same as the complement of the probability of J_2 and O_2. That is $P(J_1 \text{ or } O_1) = 1 - P(J_2 \text{ and } O_2)$.

$$1 - P(J_2 \text{ and } O_2)$$

	J_1	J_2	$P(O_i)$
O_1	0.30	0.15	0.45
O_2	0.20	0.35	0.55
$P(J_i)$	0.50	0.50	1.00

$$P(J_1 \text{ or } O_1) = 1 - P(J_2 \cap O_2) = 1 - 0.35 = 0.65$$

From the above two possible ways, the probability that the event J_1 or O_1 occurs can be found using their marginal probabilities as, $P(J_1 \text{ or } O_1) = P(J_1) + P(O_1) - P(J_1 \cap O_1)$.

	J_1	J_2	$P(O_i)$
O_1	0.30	0.15	0.45
O_2	0.20	0.35	0.55
$P(J_i)$	0.50	0.50	1.00

$$P(J_1 \text{ or } O_1) = P(J_1) + P(O_1) - P(J_1 \cap O_1) = 0.50 + 0.45$$
$$- 0.30 = 0.65$$

This example leads to the addition rule of probability. If M and N are two events, then the probability that M or N occurs is P(M or N) = P(MN)=P(M)+P(N) - P(M∩N).

Thus, there are three rules of probability. The complement rule gives the probability of an event not occurring. The complement of an event M is M^c. Then, $P(M^c)=1 - P(M)$. The product rule or multiplication rule is given by conditional probability and is used to calculate the joint probability of two events. For the events M and N, the joint probability is P(M and N) = P(M∩N) = P(M|N)P(N) = P(N|M)P(M). The addition rule is given by marginal probabilities, joint probabilities, and/or complement probabilities. For the events M and N the addition rule is P(M or N) = P(MN)=P(M)+P(N)-P(M∩N).

Example

A, B and C are three delivery services operating in a small town in Karnataka. Service A manages 60 per cent,

Service B manages 30 per cent and Service C manages the remaining 10 per cent of the scheduled deliveries in the town. On-time delivery rates of these delivery services A, B and C respectively are 80 per cent, 60 per cent and 40 per cent. Let O represent on-time delivery and L denote late delivery. Note that L = O^c. The probabilities given in this problem can be written as:

P(A)=0.60
P(B)=0.30
P(C)=0.10
P(O|A)=0.80 => $P(O^c|A)$=P(L|A)=0.20
P(O|B)=0.60 => $P(O^c|B)$=P(L|A)=0.40
P(O|C)=0.40 => $P(O^c|C)$=P(L|A)=0.60

From the given marginal and conditional probabilities, the joint probabilities can be found. The conditional probability P(O|A)=P(A and O)/P(A). Cross multiplying this gives P(A and O) = P(O|A)P(A). Similarly, the other joint probabilities P(B and O) and P(C and O) can be obtained.

P(A and O) = P(O|A)P(A) = (0.80)(0.6) = 0.48
P(A and O^c) = $P(O^c|A)$P(A) = (0.20)(0.6) = 0.12
P(B and O) = P(O|B)P(B) = (0.60)(0.30) = 0.18
P(B and O^c) = $P(O^c|B)$P(B) = (0.40)(0.3) = 0.12
P(C and O) = P(O|C)P(C) = (0.40)(0.1) = 0.04
P(Cand O^c) = $P(O^c|C)$P(C) = (0.60)(0.10) = 0.06

The probabilities can be represented by a contingency table.

	A	B	C	Total
O	0.48	0.18	0.04	0.70
L	0.12	0.12	0.06	0.30
Total	0.60	0.30	0.10	1.00

Using the above probabilities, the other probabilities are found. If a package was delivered on time, the probability that it was Service B is P(B|O)=P(B and O)/P(O) = 0.18 / 0.70 = 0.257. If a package was delivered on time, the probability that it was Service C is P(C|O)=P(C and O)/P(O) = 0.04/0.70 = 0.057. If a package was delivered 40 minutes late, the probability that it was Service A is P(A|L)=P(A and L) / P(L) = (0.60)(0.20)/0.30 = 0.40. If a package was delivered forty minutes late, the probability that it was Service B is P(B|L) = P(B and L)/P(L) = P(L|B)P(B)/P(L) = (0.30)(0.40)/0.30 = 0.40. If a package was delivered 40 minutes late, the probability that it was Service C is P(C|L) = P(C and L)/P(L) = (0.10)(0.60) /0.30 = 0.20.

Example

A, B and C are three popular hospitals in a city. Let P(A), P(B) and P(C) are the probabilities of patients treated in the hospitals A, B and C respectively. The history of these three hospitals show that P(A) = 0.5, P(B) =

0.3, P(C) = 0.2. The probabilities of a malpractice suit being filed given that a patient is treated in one of these three hospitals are P(M|A)=0.001, P(M|B)=0.005, and P(M|C)=0.008. Accordingly, the probabilities that a malpractice suit is *not* filed given that a patient is treated in one of these three hospitals are P(M^c|A)=0.999, P(M^c|B)=0.995 and P(M^c|C)=0.992.

From the given marginal and conditional probabilities, the joint probabilities can be found. The conditional probability P(M|A) = P(A and M)/P(A). Cross multiplying this gives P(A and M) = P(M|A)P(A). Similarly, the other joint probabilities P(B and M) and P(C and M) can be obtained.

P(A and M) = P(M|A)P(A) = (0.001)(0.5) = 0.0005
P(A and M^c) = P(M^c|A)P(A) = (0.999)(0.5) = 0.4995
P(B and M) = P(M|B)P(B) = (0.005)(0.30) = 0.0015
P(B and M^c) = P(M^c|B)P(B) = (0.995)(0.3) = 0.2985
P(C and M) = P(M|C)P(C) = (0.008)(0.2) = 0.0016
P(Cand M^c) = P(M^c|C)P(C) = (0.992)(0.20) = 0.1984

	A	B	C	Total
M	0.0005	0.0015	0.0016	0.0036
M^c	0.4995	0.2985	0.1984	0.9964
Total	0.50	0.30	0.20	1.00

Using the above probabilities, the other conditional probabilities can be found. If a malpractice suit is filed, the probability that the patient was treated in Hospital

A is P(A|M)=P(A and M)/P(M) = 0.0005/0.0036 = 0.001389. If a malpractice suit is filed, the probability that the patient was treated in Hospital B is P(B|M)=P(B and M)/P(M) = 0.0015/0.0036 = 0.4167. If a malpractice suit is filed, the probability that the patient was treated in Hospital C is P(C|M)=P(C and M)/P(M) = 0.0016/0.0036 = 0.4444. If no malpractice suit is filed, the probability that the patient was treated in Hospital A is P(A|M^c)=P(A and M^c)/P(M^c) = 0.4995/0.9964 = 0.5013. If no malpractice suit is filed, the probability that the patient was treated in Hospital B is P(B|M^c)=P(B and M^c)/P(M^c) = 0.2985/0.9964 = 0.2996. If no malpractice suit is filed, the probability that the patient was treated in Hospital C is P(C|M^c)=P(C and M^c)/P(M^c) = 0.1984/0.9964 = 0.1991.

Bayes' theorem

The computation of probabilities as in the examples discussed led to a popular theorem called Bayes' theorem, introduced by Thomas Bayes. The marginal probabilities are usually known as prior probabilities and the conditional probabilities are known as posterior probabilities. These posterior probabilities show how the marginal probabilities change if additional information is available on the events. The statement of Bayes' theorem is:

$$P(N|M) = P(M|N)P(N)/P(M)$$

In case P(M) is not known, the same can be computed using $P(M)=P(M|N)P(N)+P(M|N^c)P(N^c)$.

In this case Bayes' theorem is stated as:

$$P(N|M)=P(M|N)P(N)/\ [P(M|N)P(N)+P(M|N^c)P(N^c)].$$

From the probabilities, it may also be seen that $P(M)=P(M$ and $N) + P(M$ and $N^c)$. Hence, $P(M|N)$ $= P(M|N)P(N)/[P(M$ and $N) + P(M$ and $N^c]$. Bayes' theorem helps find the posterior probabilities given the marginal and conditional probabilities.

Example

A fruit basket has 7 mangoes and 3 apples. A person consumes two fruits a day from the basket. What is the probability that two apples are consumed in a day?

Let A represent the event an apple is consumed and M is the event a mango is consumed. $P(A) = 3/10$ and $P(M) = 7/10$. Let F_1 be the first fruit consumed and F_2 be the second fruit consumed. Then $P(F_1) = P(A) = 3/10$. The probability that the second fruit consumed is an apple given the first fruit consumed is an apple is $P(F_2=Apple|F_1=Apple) = 2/9$. Then, the probability that two apples are consumed in a day is found using the multiplication rule as $P(F_1=Apple$ and $F_2=Apple)$ $= P(F_1=Apple) \bullet P(F_2=Apple|F_1=Apple) = (3/10)(2/9) = 6/90 = 1/15$.

Example

A fruit basket has 7 mangoes and 3 apples. A person consumes one fruit every day from the basket. The basket is replenished at the end of each day so that every day there are 7 mangoes and 3 apples. What is the probability that the person consumes apples for two consecutive days?

Let A represent the event an apple is consumed and M be the event a mango is consumed. $P(A) = 3/10$ and $P(M) = 7/10$. Let F1 be the fruit consumed on day one and F2 be the fruit consumed on day two. Then $P(F_1) = P(A) = 3/10 = 0.30$. The probability that the fruit consumed on the second day is an apple given that the fruit consumed on the previous day is an apple $P(F_2=Apple|F_1=Apple) = P(F_2=Apple) = P(A) = 3/10 = 0.30$. The probability of consuming an apple on the second day is independent of consuming an apple on previous day. $P(F_1=Apple$ and $F_2=Apple) = P(F_1=Apple) \bullet P(F_2=Apple|F_1=Apple) = P(F_1=Apple) \bullet P(F_2=Apple) = (3/10)(3/10) = 9/100 = 0.09$.

Mutually exclusive events and independent events

A fruit basket has 7 mangoes and 3 apples. A person consumes a fruit every day from the basket. The basket is replenished at the end of each day so that every day there are 7 mangoes and 3 apples. Let A represent the event an apple is consumed and M is the event a mango is consumed. P(A) = 3/10 and P(M) = 7/10. If one fruit is taken from the basket, then P(A∩M) = 0. That is, A and M are mutually exclusive. As the P(A)•P(M) = (3/10)•(7/10) ≠ 0, P(A)•P(M) ≠ P(A∩M). Hence A and M are not independent. Mutually exclusive events are not necessarily independent. Independent events cannot be mutually exclusive unless the probability of one of the events is zero.

Random variable

Human life is built around random experiments. In real-life situations, knowingly or unknowingly, probabilities are assigned and decisions are made at every instance. Understanding the patterns of such instances of random events helps in predictive modelling of such occurrences. A basic need is to create meaningful measurements for the events. Recollect the software development problem explained at the beginning of this chapter. The events of this experiment are the total project completion times, which can be represented by a set S = (8, 9, 10, 11, 12) where each element in this set is either an elementary unit or a combination of the elementary units. If X is a variable that represents the total project completion time, it can take values like 8, 9, 10, 11 and 12. For example, the completion time 8 is given by a single outcome (2, 6) as shown in the tree diagram. Hence, a probability of 1/9 is assigned to this outcome. Similarly, the completion time 10 is given by the outcomes (2, 8), (3, 7) and (4, 6), and hence a probability of 3/9 is assigned to this event. Likewise, probabilities can be assigned to each event. Thus, a variable X (total project completion time) is created, which takes the possible values 8, 9, 10, 11 and 12, and for each possible value X takes, there is a probability associated. Understand that variable X is not an ordinary variable. To understand this better, it is necessary to know what a function is.

Consider a kindergarten school. The mothers send their children to the school early in the morning with a lunch box either by school bus or private transport or they are dropped off by fathers on their way to office. The proud mothers make it a practice to pick up their children after school. The mothers reach the gate of the school at least ten minutes before the school bell rings and wait outside the gate. The school management keeps the main gate closed to prevent the mothers from entering and disturbing the ongoing classes. As soon as the school bell rings, ending the school day, the children run out of their classes towards the main gate and go to their mothers shouting, *Hi mom . . . Hi mom . . .* This is an emotional moment every day at school. Each child runs up to its mother. One child or more than one child may run to one mother (if the mother has more than one child studying in the school) and in no case will one child run up to more than one mother saying *Hi mom . . .* This is called a function. This scenario is explained in the figure below.

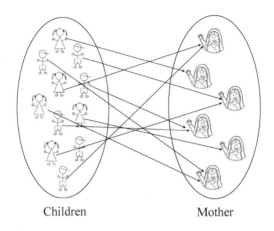

Children   Mother

The above is a mapping of children to the mother. The mapping is one-to-one and many-to-one. This is a typical example of a function. Similarly, the function with random experiments can be created, which helps in understanding the patterns in the data. Consider the simple random experiment of tossing an unbiased (fair) coin.

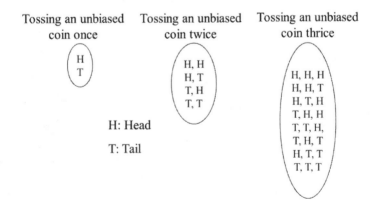

Tossing an unbiased coin once	Tossing an unbiased coin twice	Tossing an unbiased coin thrice
H T	H, H H, T T, H T, T	H, H, H H, H, T H, T, H T, H, H T, T, H, T, H, T H, T, T T, T, T

H: Head

T: Tail

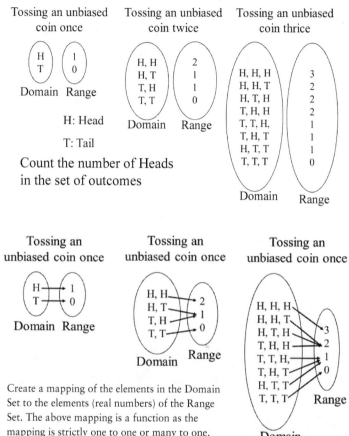

Tossing an unbiased coin once

H: Head

T: Tail

Count the number of Heads in the set of outcomes

Create a mapping of the elements in the Domain Set to the elements (real numbers) of the Range Set. The above mapping is a function as the mapping is strictly one to one or many to one.

Let X represent the number of heads. From the three consecutive figures, it can be seen that X is a real-valued function mapping the elements of the random experiments to unique elements of the set of real numbers. This means assigning a real number to each of the elements of the sample space or outcome of a random experiment. This leads to the definition of the random variable as a real-valued function that maps the elements of the sample space to the set of real numbers (or) a real-valued function that assigns a numerical number for the very outcome of a random experiment.

Upper-case letters like X, Y and Z are used to represent random variables. Lower-case letters like x, y and z are used to represent the values of the random variable.

Discrete random variable

A random variable that always takes integer values is a discrete random variable. In the coin-tossing example, the number of heads is a discrete random variable.

Probability distribution function

A probability distribution function is a mathematical expression $P(X=x)$ that shows the probability of each value of X. Probability distribution distributes probabilities to all possible values a discrete random variable can take. Let X be a random variable with possible values $x_1, x_2, \ldots, x_n$. A probability distribution function $P(X=x) = P(x)$ shows the probability for each value x of X. Note that $0 \leq P(x) \leq 1$, and $\sum_1^n P(x_i) = 1$.

Example

The table below gives the number of desktop computers sold per week by a computer shop in a small city over seventy weeks. This is a case of a discrete probability distribution.

Number of desktop computers sold in a week	Number of weeks	Probability (relative frequency)
25	2	0.0286
26	7	0.1000
27	11	0.1571
28	19	0.2714
29	12	0.1714
30	9	0.1286
31	6	0.0857
32	4	0.0571

The probability distribution of a discrete random variable can be shown using a histogram.

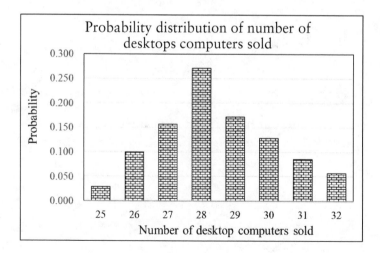

Cumulative probability distribution

A cumulative probability distribution function $P(X \leq x)$ shows the cumulative sum of probabilities, adding from the smallest to the largest value of X, gradually approaching unity.

The cumulative probability distribution of the number of desktop computers sold in a week by a computer shop in a small city over seventy weeks is given in the table below.

Number of desktop computers sold in a week	Number of weeks	Probability (Relative frequency)	Cumulative Probability
25	2	0.0286	0.0286
26	7	0.1000	0.1286
27	11	0.1571	0.2857
28	19	0.2714	0.5571
29	12	0.1714	0.7286
30	9	0.1286	0.8571
31	6	0.0857	0.9429
32	4	0.0571	1.0000

The cumulative probability distribution of this discrete random variable can be shown using a histogram.

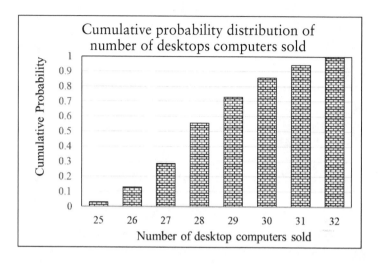

Average or expected value

If X is a discrete random variable, then the expected value $E(X)$ or the average value of X is the sum of all the values of X weighted by their respective probabilities. If there are n distinct values of X, say x_1, x_2, . . ., x_n, then $EX = \sum x_i P(x_i)$. $E(X)$ is a measure of the central tendency. It can be verified that, when $P(x_i) = 1/n$ for all x_i, the expected value becomes $EX = \frac{1}{n}\sum x_i$, which is the arithmetic mean.

Example

A pharmaceutical sales representative makes about seven marketing visits on any given day. The probability distribution of his sales visits per day is:

x	0	1	2	3	4	5	6	7	Total
P(x)	0.03	0.05	0.10	0.25	0.30	0.18	0.07	0.02	1.00

The expected number (average) of marketing visits is computed as:

x	0	1	2	3	4	5	6	7	Total
P(x)	0.03	0.05	0.10	0.25	0.30	0.18	0.07	0.02	1.00
xP(x)	0	0.05	0.20	0.75	1.20	0.90	0.42	0.14	3.66

The sum of the xP(x) column is the expected value or the average of the discrete distribution. The expected value is 3.66. The average number of marketing visits is 3.66. It may be meaningfully concluded that the pharmaceutical sales representative makes about four marketing visits per day on average. The probability distribution can be represented by a histogram.

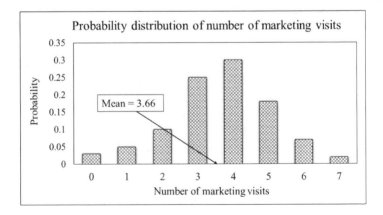

This particular probability distribution is almost symmetric around the mean $\mu = 3.66$. The mean is the balancing point or fulcrum. Because $E(X)$ is an average, it does not have to be an observable point.

In real-life business situations, one comes across several random experiments and associated probability distributions based on which decisions are made. Expected value plays an important role in arriving at certain significant solutions. Life insurance companies continuously estimate and work with this kind of probability distribution. Consider a simple example of fixing the premium for term life insurance.

Example

A life insurance company continuously monitors the mortality rate of people in a specific region of the country. The history of the region shows that the probability that a person aged above forty years will die within the next year is 0.001. If a person aged forty-five years wishes to take a one-year term policy of Rs 50,00,000, what premium should the life insurance company charge on this policy?

Let X be the amount paid by the company to settle the policy in case of the death of the person. Then the expected amount to be paid is computed as the expected value of X.

Event	x	P(x)	xP(x)
Live	0	0.999	0
Die	50,00,000	0.001	5000
Total		1.00000	5000

From the computations, it is seen that the expected amount to be paid to settle the Rs 50,00,000 one-year term policy is Rs 5000. This Rs 5000 is the break-even value. The life insurance company may charge a premium of Rs 5000 plus the cost of administrative expenses and desired profit.

Example

During the festival season, in a mall in Bengaluru, lucky dip coupons are sold at Rs 250 per coupon with a jackpot prize of a car worth Rs 30,00,000. It is learned that in that season, 13,500 coupons are sold before the draw of the lucky dip. Was the cost of Rs 250 per coupon justified?

This can be verified by calculating the expected amount to be paid to give away the jackpot prize based on the probability of a winning coupon. The price of a coupon is Rs 250 to win a new car worth Rs 30,00,000. Given that 13,500 coupons are sold, the probability of a winning coupon is 1/23,500. The expected value of the amount to be paid to settle the prize is:

Event	x	P(x)	xP(x)
Win	30,00, 000	1/13,500	222.22
Lose	0	1/13,499	0
Total		1.00000	222.22

The expected amount to be paid to settle the prize of a car worth Rs 30,00,000 is Rs 222.22. This is the break-even value of the coupon. The price of the coupon is usually fixed at break-even cost plus the return to cover the administrative expenses and profit. Hence the price of Rs 250 may be considered justified.

Variance

The tendency of data to cluster around a value at the centre leads to the concept of dispersion. The expected value is the average value that is expected to lie at the centre. To study the extent the data points deviate from this average, the deviations from the average are used. The use of squared deviations from the average was explained in the second chapter. There is also an expected value for these squared deviations from the average. The expected value of these squared deviations is the variance.

Suppose there are n distinct values of X, say x_1, x_2, . . ., x_n. Then the variance of the discrete random variable X is the weighted average of the dispersion about the mean, $V(X) = \sigma^2 = \sum_1^n \left(x_i - \mu \right)^2 P(x_i)$. Here μ is the population mean. The standard deviation is the square root of the variance and is denoted by σ. It can be easily seen that when $P(x_i)=1/n$, $V(X)$ reduces to $\frac{1}{n}\sum_1^n(x_i-\mu)^2$, the one given in chapter 2.

Example

The example below illustrates the use of the expected value and standard deviation of a probability distribution.

A homestay in Coorg, Karnataka, has five guest rooms. The occupancy rate of the homestay in the past is given in the table. Let X be the random variable, the number of rooms occupied.

x	0	1	2	3	4	5
P(x)	0.05	0.15	0.25	0.35	0.12	0.08

The expected number and the variance of the rooms occupied are computed as:

x	P(x)	x P(x)	$(x-\mu)^2$ P(x)
0	0.05	0	0.33282
1	0.15	0.15	0.37446
2	0.25	0.5	0.0841
3	0.35	1.05	0.06174
4	0.12	0.48	0.24197
5	0.08	0.4	0.46851
Total	1.00	$\mu = 2.58$	$\sigma^2 = 1.5636$ 1.5636

The standard deviation $\sigma = \sqrt{1.5636} = 1.2504$. The expected value and the standard deviation are two important measures, the combination of which helps understand the behaviour of the random variable and in decision-making. The average number of rooms occupied is 2.58 with a standard deviation of 1.2504 rooms. This indicates that on average, 3 rooms are occupied. The standard deviation indicates there is a considerable amount of variation in the number of rooms occupied. Another descriptive measure, the mode, helps in decision-making. The mode of the number of rooms occupied is three as the highest probability of 0.35 is against three rooms. Incidentally, the mode and the mean coincide. This reveals that the homestay on average is doing reasonably well, assuming 40 per cent occupancy is the break-even.

The histogram below explains the distribution of the room occupancy.

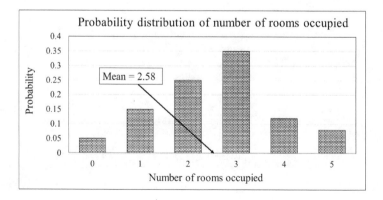

Bernoulli distribution

Bernoulli distribution is the basic and simple discrete probability distribution that is mathematically formulated. A random experiment with only two outcomes is a Bernoulli experiment. One outcome is designated as a success with a probability of success p, while the other is designated as a failure with a probability of failure *(1-p)*. In practice, the outcome that is less likely to occur is considered a success. P(Success) + P(Failure) = p + (1–p) = 1 and $0 \leq p \leq 1$. For ease of application and mathematical treatment, the Bernoulli random variable, say X, is assumed to take the numerical value 1 for success and 0 for failure. Thus, the probability distribution of Bernoulli is:

Outcome	X = x	Probability P(x)
Success	1	p
Failure	0	1-p

From the probability distribution of Bernoulli, the mean and variance are derived as:

$$E(X) = \sum_{1}^{2} x_i P\left(x_i\right) = 0 \cdot (1-p) + 1 \cdot p = p$$

$$V(X) = \sum_{1}^{n} \left(x_i - EX\right)^2 P(xi) = (1-p)^2 p + (0-p)^2 (1-p) = p(1-p)$$

A few examples of Bernoulli's experiment are:

a) Flipping a coin
b) Examining a television screen for a crack
c) Testing for the presence of a virus
d) Conversion of a sales call
e) Classification of a manufactured product as defective or non-defective
f) Paying or not paying by credit card
g) The outcome of a surgery
h) A service is late or not late
i) On time or not on time
j) Pass or fail

Binomial distribution

The binomial distribution is derived as a special case of the Bernoulli distribution. Suppose that a Bernoulli experiment is repeated n times. Each Bernoulli trial is independent so that the probability of success 'p' remains constant. The outcomes are successes and failures. Assume X_1, X_2, . . ., X_n are the outcomes of the 'n' Bernoulli trials. Each of these X_i takes the numerical value 1 or 0 depending on whether it is a success or failure.

Let the random variable X represent the number of successes in the n Bernoulli trials. Then, the random variable $X = X_1 + X_2 + . . . + X_n$. In binomial distribution, the interest is finding the probability of 'x' successes (x≤n) in 'n' Bernoulli trials. That is $P(X=x)$. It is easy to visualize the mathematical form of the binomial distribution as there are n places available for x successes with the probability of success p and the probability of failure (1-p). The x successes out of n trials can come in ^nC_x possible ways, the probability of x successes is p multiplied x times, which is p^x, and the probability of n-x failures is (1-p) multiplied (n-x) times, which is $(1-p)^{n-x}$.

Hence, the binomial probability distribution of finding x successes in Bernoulli trials is $P(X=x) = P(x) = {}^nC_x p^x (1-p)^{n-x}$ for x=0, 1, 2, . . ., n. As the binomial distribution is a result of n independent Bernoulli trials, the mean of the binomial distribution is found by adding the means for each of the n Bernoulli independent trials. That is, the mean of binomial distribution is p+p+ . . . +p = np. Similarly, the variance of the binomial distribution is p(1-p)+ p(1-p) + . . . + p(1-p) = np(1-p). The standard deviation is $\sqrt{np(1-p)}$. The binomial distribution is thus characterized by the two parameters n and p. The binomial distribution is skewed right if p<0.50, skewed left if p>0.50, and symmetric if p=0.50. The skew-ness decreases as n increases, regardless of the value of p.

The exact binomial probabilities, $P(X=x)$, can be computed using the Excel code BINOM.DIST(k,n,p,0) and the cumulative binomial probabilities, $P(X≤x)$, can be computed using the Excel code BINOM.DIST(k,n,p,1).

Examples of binomial distribution

Food delivery

Consider a food delivery service, Zomato. Zomato needs to ensure that the service time is not considered late by any customer. Service times are defined as either late or not late (Bernoulli). Let X be the number of food orders that are served late out of the total number of food orders served. Food orders are independent of each other. Zomato has a reputation that only 8 per cent of the food orders are served late. The probability of a late service is consistent and is equal to 0.08.

The probability that exactly two of the next n=15 food orders served being late is $P(X=2) = P(2) = 15c_x(0.08)^2(0.92)^{13}$ = BINOM.DIST(2,15,0.08,0) = 0.227306068. The probability of not more than two of the next ten food orders served being late is $P(X\leq2)$= BINOM.DIST(2,10,0.08,1) = 0.95992458. The probability of more than one of the next ten food orders served are late is $1-P(X\leq1)$= 1-BINOM.DIST(2,10,0.08,1) = 0.04007542.

Poisson distribution

An interesting random experiment involving the occurrence of rare events was described by the French mathematician Siméon Denis Poisson (1781–1840). Siméon, while observing a special kind of random experiment in which the opportunity for occurrences of events is very high, but the actual occurrences are very few, conceived this discrete distribution, which was later named after him as the Poisson distribution. Consider an ordinary A4 size white paper. The A4 size is approximately 8.3 inches by 11.7 inches. The white surface of the paper may contain a few black dots, brown dots, wood particles or even small holes, which are known as blemishes. The number of blemishes can be as high as infinite, but, due to stringent quality control activities, they are contained to be very few. Now consider the number of airplanes in flight. There can be a few thousand airplanes in the sky at any given point in time leading to a very high opportunity for air accidents/collisions. But in real-time such accidents are almost nil.

Similarly, the number of road accidents at a junction on a busy road in a short interval of time between 9 a.m. and 9.10 a.m., the number of customers arriving at a fuel station, the number of persons arriving at an ATM at a given interval of time, the number of trauma patients arriving at a hospital between 7 p.m. and 7.30 p.m., etc., are all examples of Poisson events. People write blogs and post YouTube videos regularly. The subscriptions to the blogs or YouTube videos are Poisson events. Supposing on average, twelve new people subscribe to someone's YouTube channel per week, then it would be of interest to see what the probability is of twenty people subscribing in the next week.

The Poisson distribution describes the number of occurrences of such rare events within a randomly chosen unit of time or space, say within a minute, hour, day, square foot or mile. The Poisson distribution is also known as the model of arrivals. Arrivals (e.g., customers, defects, accidents) are independent of each other. The Poisson random variable X is the number of events or occurrences per unit of time. As the number of events that can occur in a given unit of time is not bounded, the random variable X has no obvious limit. The Poisson probabilities taper off toward zero as X increases.

The mathematical form of the probability distribution is visualized by fixing the average occurrences per unit of time, say λ. $P(X = x) = P(x) = \dfrac{e^{-\lambda}\lambda^x}{x!}$, x=0, 1, 2, . . . While the mean of the Poisson distribution is fixed at λ, the variance V(X) is derived from the relation $V(X)=E(X-EX)^2 = \sum_x (x-\lambda)^2 \cdot \dfrac{e^{-\lambda}\lambda^x}{x!} = \lambda$. The mean and variance of the Poisson distribution are the same. As Poisson is a model of rare events, the λ is expected to be less than or equal to twenty. Poisson distribution is always right-skewed; skew-ness reduces for larger values of λ. The exact Poisson probabilities, P(X=x), can be computed using the Excel code POISSON.DIST(x,λ,0), and the cumulative Poisson probabilities, P(X≤x), can be computed using the Excel code POISSON.DIST(x,λ,1).

The Poisson distribution is also visualized as a limiting case of the binomial distribution when the number of trials n increases indefinitely whilst the product np= λ, which is the expected value of the number of successes from the trials, remains constant. This helps in determining binomial probabilities as a special case.

Examples of Poisson distribution

Highway congestion

It is observed that, on average, 240 cars per hour pass a specified point on an express highway during the morning rush hour. Due to some repair works on the road it is estimated that congestion will occur closer to the city centre if more than five cars pass the point in any one minute. The possibility of congestion can be computed using the Poisson distribution. Here λ = 4 cars per minute. The probability of more than 5 cars passing the point in any one minute is P(X>5) = 1-P(X≤5) = POISSON.DIST(5,4,1) = 0.21487. There is approximately a 22 per cent chance of congestion at any one minute.

Insurance claims

An insurance company decides on the premium amount based on the number of claims and the amount claimed per year. To evaluate the premium amount, the insurance company will calculate the average amount paid off per year in settling claims. This depends on the average number of claims filed in the year. Assuming on average five claims are handled by an insurance company per day, the probability of ten claims per day is POISSON.DIST(10,5,0) = 0.18133. The probability of more than ten claims per day is 1-POISSON.DIST(10,5,1) = 0.013695. The probability of between 15 to 25 claims per day is POISSON.DIST(25,5,1)-POISSON.DIST(15,5,1) = 0.000069. The probability of fewer than 8 claims per day is POISSON.DIST(7,5,1) = 0.9319064.

Continuous distribution

For a discrete probability distribution, each value of a random variable carries its probability, $P(x)$. In a continuous distribution, the events are intervals (the random variables take values in an interval) and probabilities are areas underneath smooth curves. The random variable cannot assume an integer value and hence the probability of a continuous random variable assuming a specific integer value is zero.

The probability distribution function $f(x)$ of a continuous random variable is an equation that shows the height of the curve $f(x)$ at each possible value of X over the range of X. The cumulative distribution function is denoted by $F(x)=P(X\leq x)$.

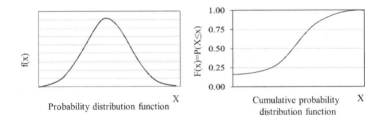

Probability distribution function

Cumulative probability distribution function

As continuous random variables do not assume any specific value, the probability (calculated as area) at any single point is zero. The probability that the random variable takes a value in an interval (a, b) is the area under the curve in the interval and is found by integration f(x).

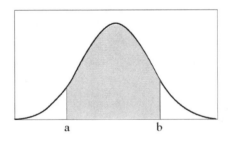

The expected value and the variance of a continuous random variable are defined in similar terms to the discrete random variable.

$$E(X) = \mu = \int_{-\infty}^{\infty} xf(x)dx, \text{ and}$$

$$V(X) = \sigma^2 = \int_{-\infty}^{\infty} (x-\mu)^2 f(x)dx.$$

Several instances of normal behaviour were discussed in chapter 1. A data set in which most of the values cluster around a central value, with values tapering off as they go further away from the centre, is said to have a normal distribution. In a normal distribution, data is symmetrically distributed with no skew-ness. The measures of central tendency (mean, mode and median) are the same in a normal distribution. The four properties, namely symmetric, unimodal, asymptotic and the coinciding mean, median and mode characterize a normal distribution. A normal distribution is perfectly symmetrical around its centre. Exactly half of the values are to the left of the centre and exactly half the values are to the right. Every natural phenomenon follows normal distribution if not affected by external factors.

Normal distribution or Gaussian distribution

Normal or Gaussian distribution was named after the German mathematician Karl Gauss (1777–1855). The mathematical function of the normal distribution was derived by fixing the mean μ, and the standard deviation σ. The mean defines the fulcrum, and the standard deviation defines the inflection point of the normal curve. The normal distribution is defined by the two parameters, μ and σ, and is denoted by $N(\mu, \sigma)$. The normal random variable is defined in the interval $-\infty < X < \infty$.

The probability distribution function or the probability density function of a normal random variable is:

$$f(x) = \frac{1}{\sqrt{2\pi}\sigma}\, e^{-\frac{1}{2}\left(\frac{x-\mu}{\sigma}\right)^2}, -\infty < x < \infty.$$

The mean and variance are designated as μ and σ^2. The cumulative normal probabilities can be computed using the Excel code, NORM.DIST(x, μ, σ, 1), using which the probabilities in intervals can be obtained. The normal distribution serves as a benchmark to compare other distributions.

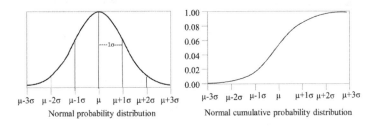

Normal probability distribution   Normal cumulative probability distribution

Normal probability density function $f(x)$ reaches a maximum at μ and has points of inflection at $\mu+\sigma$. Almost all the area under the normal curve is included in the interval $[(\mu-3\sigma), (\mu+3\sigma)]$. All normal distributions have the same shape but differ in the scales of the axes.

Since for every combination of μ and σ there is a different normal distribution, it is practically difficult to visualize and use the probability density functions. Also, until recently, computing the probabilities has been a challenge. Now, one can compute normal probabilities with the help of computers, such as by using Excel codes. However, there has been a need to have a common probability density function for any normal random variable irrespective of the numerical measurements and to simplify the computation of normal probabilities. A transformation of a normal random variable to a standard normal distribution by a substitution $z = \dfrac{X-\mu}{\sigma}$ was evolved. The distribution of Z, which has a mean $\mu=0$ and standard deviation $\sigma=1$, is called a standard normal distribution. Irrespective of any X, the distribution of Z is the same. The probability density function of Z simplifies to

$$f(z) = \frac{1}{\sqrt{2\pi}}\, e^{-\frac{z^2}{2}}, \; -\infty < z < \infty.$$

The cumulative normal probabilities can be computed using the Excel code NORM.S.DIST(z,1), using which the probabilities in intervals can be obtained.

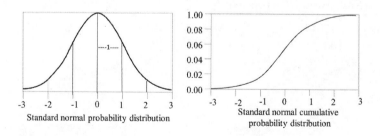

Standard normal probability distribution

Standard normal cumulative probability distribution

In the normal distribution and the standard normal distribution, the interval $\pm\, 2\sigma$ from the mean includes approximately 95 per cent of the area under the curve and the interval ± 3σ from the mean includes approximately 99.7 per cent of the area under the curve.

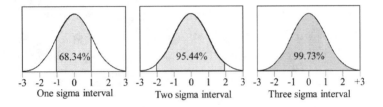

One sigma interval   Two sigma interval   Three sigma interval

Several tables giving standard normal probabilities are available for computing probabilities. However, the use of such tables has become obsolete as the probabilities are easily computed using simple Excel codes as well as other languages and software.

Examples of normal distribution

Poverty

Suppose the annual family income in a given region is normally distributed with a mean of Rs 5,00,000 and a standard deviation of Rs 2,00,000. If the poverty level is Rs 1,00,000, then the population that lives in poverty is

$$P(X \leq 100000) = \text{NORM.DIST}(100000, 500000, 200000, 1) = 0.02275013.$$

That is, about 2.3 per cent of the population lives in poverty. Using the standard normal distribution,

$$Z = (100000-500000)/200000 = -2$$

The required population that lives in poverty is

$$P(Z \leq -2) = \text{NORM.S.DIST}(-2,1) = 0.02275013.$$

Piston rings

Mechanical piston rings are usually produced in bulk. Historical data shows that the average internal diameter is 60 mm and the standard deviation is 0.02 mm. If the acceptable range is 59.95 mm to 60.05 mm, the proportion of output that is acceptable is NORM.DIST(60.05, 60,0.02,1) - NORM.DIST(59.95,60,0.02,1) = 0.98758067. The same using the standard normal distribution is, NORM.S.DIST(2.5,1) - NORM.S.DIST(-2.5,1) = 0.98758067. That is, about 99 per cent of the output would meet the acceptance criterion.

Normal approximation to binomial and Poisson probabilities

Often, computing binomial and Poisson probabilities can be tedious, and it may not be possible to compute them accurately due to factorial operation, especially when the number of trials n is large. The binomial distribution becomes symmetric for large values of n and the Poisson distribution becomes symmetric when λ is large ($\lambda \geq 10$). Under circumstances when n is large so that np $\geq$ 5 and n(1-p) $\geq$ 5, it is acceptable to use the normal approximation to the binomial by setting np=μ and $\sqrt{(np(1-p))}=\sigma$. Under circumstances when λ is large ($\lambda \geq 10$), it is acceptable to use the normal approximation to the Poisson by setting $\lambda=\mu$ and $\sqrt{\lambda}=\sigma$.

Example – binomial to normal

In a city, 55 per cent of the population favours a new tax scheme of the government. Suppose a sample inquiry of 600 citizens is conducted. The probability that at least 300 of the sampled citizens favour the new tax scheme of the government

a) using the binomial distribution is 1-BINOM. DIST(299,600,0.55,1) = 0.993746798
b) using normal distribution is 1- NORM.DIST(299, 330,12.186058,1) = 0.994518731

Example—Poisson to normal

On average, twenty-two calls per hour are received in a customer-care centre of a mobile network company. The probability of receiving more than twenty-five calls

a) using the Poisson distribution is 1-POISSON. DIST(25,22,1) = 0.222900852

b) using normal distribution is 1- NORM.DIST(25, 22, 4.69041576,1) = 0.26121564.

Exponential distribution

While the occurrences of events per unit of time follow the Poisson distribution, the time between two occurrences of Poisson events follows the exponential distribution. The time between two occurrences is a continuous variable, taking values greater than zero. Waiting time or time between occurrences of two Poisson events is exponential. If the number of arrivals per unit of time is a Poisson distribution with an average λ, then the random variable 'X', the time between two arrivals, or the waiting time before the next event happens follows the exponential distribution with the probability distribution function,

$$f(x) = \lambda e^{-\lambda x}, \; x > 0.$$

The cumulative probability distribution function is:

$$F(x) = P(X \leq x) = 1 - e^{-\lambda x}$$

If the random variable X represents the time between two arrivals or the waiting time with a mean of λ minutes, then the probability distribution function is:

$$f(x) = \frac{1}{\lambda} e^{-\frac{x}{\lambda}}, \; X > 0.$$

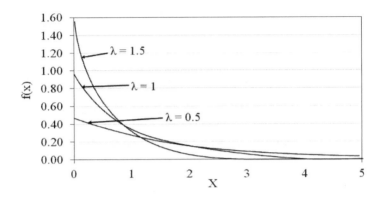

The exponential distribution is always positively skewed.

In this case, the cumulative probability distribution function is:

$$F(x) = P(X \leq x) = 1-e^{-x/\lambda}$$

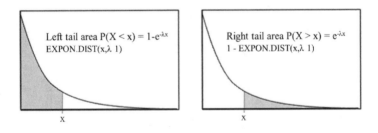

Left tail area $P(X < x) = 1-e^{-\lambda x}$
EXPON.DIST(x,λ 1)

Right tail area $P(X > x) = e^{-\lambda x}$
1 - EXPON.DIST(x,λ 1)

Patient waiting time

On average, a doctor examines five patients per hour between 4 p.m. and 8 p.m. every day. The random variable is the waiting time to see the doctor or the service time per patient. The exponential distribution is $f(x) = \dfrac{1}{12}e^{-\frac{x}{12}}$. The probability that a patient who arrives at 5.30 p.m. has to wait for at least ten minutes is $P(X>10) = e^{-10/12} = 0.434598$.

Drive-up window at a McDonald's

The time between arrivals of customers at a drive-up window of a McDonald's outlet is ten minutes. The probability that a customer arrives within seven minutes is $P(X \leq 7) = P(X < 7) = 1 - e^{-7/10} = 1 - e^{-0.7} = 0.5034146962$. The probability that a customer arrives between three to seven minutes is $P(X \leq 7) - P(X \leq 3) = [(1 - e^{-7/10}) - (1 - e^{-3/10})] = 0.2442329169$. The probability that no customer arrives within ten minutes is $P(X>10) = e^{-10/10} = 0.367879441$.

Waiting for food—memoryless property

Suppose that one has to wait for ten minutes on average to get the food served after giving an order in a restaurant. The probability that a customer will have to wait for more than fifteen minutes for their order to be served is $P(X>15) = e^{-15/10} = 0.22313016$. The probability that a customer will have to wait for more than fifteen minutes given that they are still in the restaurant after ten minutes is $P(X>15 \mid X>10) = P(X>5) = e^{-1/2} = 0.60653066$. That is, the conditional probability in exponential distribution is the individual probability itself. This is due to the important property of exponential distribution known as the memoryless property.

4

Inferential Statistics

Introduction

Statistical inference pertains to drawing inferences about an unknown population parameter(s) based on information obtained from a random sample drawn from that population. A sample is a portion of people chosen to be represent of the population. Because collecting information from the entire population is impractical due to financial and time constraints, as well as the nature of the information necessary, a sample is investigated. A blood sample, for example, to identify specific infections. In some commercial scenarios, the population itself is unknown. It is interesting to learn about populations, but data for each unit or entity is not available. When a maker of a consumer product, such as soap, a specific brand of air purifier or cooking oil wants to know how satisfied their customers are, they use sample surveys as it is hard to identify the population of users.

Sampling

Sampling is classified into probability sampling and non-probability sampling. In probability sampling, units are selected from a population with a predefined selection criterion associating a probability for each unit in the population for being selected in the sample. In non-probability sampling, the units from the population are selected without any predefined selection criterion based on probabilities of selection. Probability sampling is usually used when the population is finite. The four basic types of probability sampling are simple random sampling, stratified random sampling, systematic sampling and cluster sampling. Examples of non-probability sampling are convenience sampling, quota sampling, judgement or purposive sampling and snowball sampling.

Sampling is an integral part of human life. To buy vegetables in a vegetable market, it is often seen that people take one or two beans and break them to see if the beans are tender and fresh, break the tip of the okra to see if it is tender, hit two coconuts against each other to see if they are ripe enough and shake the coconuts to see if they have water within them. When buying rice, a customer will bite a few grains to see if the rice is fully dry, or for cooked rice, the cook will take a few grains of rice, press them between two fingers to check if the rice is cooked properly or not and so on.

Simple random sampling

Simple random sampling is the simplest sampling method applied when all the units in the population are known and the units are selected one by one with equal probability of selection at each selection. The sample units are selected using a random number-generating procedure or by lottery method after numbering all the units in the population. This procedure ensures that each unit in the population is given an equal opportunity to be selected in the sample. During sampling inspection for quality assurance, products are chosen for inspection one by one from a batch of manufactured products. To study the socio-economic status of the students in a region, a sample of students is selected one by one at random by roll numbers from a college.

Stratified random sampling

Stratified random sampling is used when the population is large and taking a simple random sample is not easy. The large population is first divided into subgroups known as strata (a stratum is a group in which all units are supposed to be homogenous concerning at least one characteristic) and simple random samples from each of the strata are selected. This ensures the representation of the entire population in the sample. Depending upon the strata sizes the samples from each stratum may also differ in size. Collectively the samples from the strata provide the required sample for the study. For example, for a family expenditure study in India, simple random samples from all the states may be drawn so that representation from the entire country is available. Here the states are strata as they comprise people who speak a common language.

Systematic sampling

In systematic sampling, units are selected systematically at regular intervals. The sampling interval is chosen to provide a required sample size. To take a sample size n from a population of size N, every kth unit from the population is selected for the sample where the constant k is approximately equal to N/n. The first unit selected corresponds to a random number from 1 to k selected using a simple random sampling method and thereafter every kth unit is selected for the sample. This is most suitable for industrial sampling for quality inspection purposes, especially when the products are manufactured by a continuous manufacturing process.

Cluster sampling

Cluster sampling is similar to stratified random sampling wherein the entire population is grouped into subgroups (clusters) such that the subgroups are similar and within a subgroup, the units are heterogeneous containing all information available in the population. A simple random sample of clusters is selected and all units in the sampled clusters are studied. Sometimes units are also sampled from each of the selected clusters using a simple random sampling procedure, which is known as two-stage cluster sampling. Cluster sampling is more efficient than a random sample, especially when the investigation spans a large geographic area. It is easier to get data from a larger number of individuals in a few villages than it is from a small number of individuals in many villages.

Convenience sampling

Convenience sampling is a method of selecting units for the sample based on availability and easy accessibility. Information from social media, online surveys, Google forms, questionnaires sent by e-mail, telephonic interviews, feedback forms, drawing 2 ml of blood for pathology tests, etc., are examples of convenience sampling. Large samples can be collected using this method. Results based on this method of sampling are usually biased. The bias can be overcome by taking large samples from the known or unknown population. A major advantage of this method is that a sample can be drawn from unknown or large populations.

Judgment or purposive sampling

Judgment or purposive sampling involves the selection of units based on the investigator's subjective judgment, based on the purpose of the collection of data. The units are included in the sample to get the required information based on the subjective judgment, based on some auxiliary information, that the selected units possess the required information. For example, to buy coconuts people often use the auxiliary information of the sound produced by hitting two coconuts together. The pre-poll and post-poll analysis interviews during elections are based on this method. Whilst this method is time and cost-effective it is prone to bias and the judgment error of the investigator.

Quota sampling

Quota sampling combines convenience with extra effort to ensure that diverse groups of the population are represented in the sample. Mostly used in market research, this method suggests using a specific quota of the subgroups of the population to be included in the sample. For example, if the information is collected from a population containing adult males, adult females, teenage boys, teenage girls and senior citizens, this method ensures specific percentages (quota) of the population belonging to these groups are included.

Ideally, the quota represents the proportions of the subgroups of the population.

Snowball sampling

Snowball sampling is a method used for unknown populations and when it is practically difficult to reach the units in the population. For example, getting information from homeless people or illegal immigrants. Sensitive data like information about people infected with HIV is tracked using the snowball sampling method. New businesses, banks and insurance companies adopt this method when they contact people to recommend possible investors or borrowers.

Statistic and estimator

A statistic is a function of the sample observations. Inferential statistics allows making an educated judgement about a population parameter based on a statistic derived from a sample of that population picked at random. An estimator is a statistic that is used to estimate a parameter of a population. The sample mean and the sample variance are estimators of the population mean and population variance respectively. Since the estimators are used to infer/generalize about the population parameter, the estimators are expected to possess certain important properties.

Point estimation

A point estimator (a statistic) is a single numerical value derived from sample observations to determine an unknown population parameter. The difference between the estimator and its expected value is the bias. An estimator is unbiased if the expected value of the estimator equals the true value of the parameter being estimated. Consistency is another property that measures how close the estimator is to the value of the parameter. An estimator is said to be consistent if it approaches the true value of the parameter when the sample size is increased.

There may be more than one unbiased and consistent estimator for a population parameter. For the population mean, the sample mean and sample median are unbiased and consistent estimators. The most efficient point estimator is the one with the least variance among all unbiased and consistent estimators. The variance is a measure of how far the estimate varies from one sample to the next. A sufficient statistic summarizes all the information in a sample about a chosen parameter. For example, the sample mean estimates the population mean. The sample mean is a sufficient statistic if it retains all the information about the population mean that was contained in the population. A sufficient statistic becomes a complete statistic if no function of it has zero expected value unless this function itself is zero.

In a business scenario, it is usually the population mean and variance that are of interest, popularly known as the world of mu (μ) and sigma (σ). There are several estimators available for the population and mean and variance. The sample mean and the sample variance meet most of the criteria of a good estimator and hence are prominently used. Assume the population contains N units and a sample of n units is considered. Then the parameters of interest of the population are $\mu = \dfrac{1}{N}\sum_{1}^{N} X_i$ and $\sigma^2 = \dfrac{1}{N}\sum_{1}^{N}\left(X_i - \mu\right)^2$. The sample mean $\bar{x} = \dfrac{1}{n}\sum_{1}^{n} x_i$ is an unbiased estimator for μ and the sample quantity $s'^2 = \dfrac{1}{n-1}\sum_{1}^{n}\left(x_i - \bar{x}\right)^2$ is unbiased for σ^2. The sample variance $s^2 = \dfrac{1}{n}\sum_{1}^{n}\left(x_i - \bar{x}\right)^2$ is not unbiased for σ^2 as $E\left(s^2\right) = \dfrac{n-1}{n}\sigma^2 \neq \sigma^2$. But, s'^2 is unbiased for σ^2 as $E\left(s'^2\right) = \sigma^2$. The difference between s'^2 and s^2 is marginal for large samples and for small samples s'^2 serves as a better estimate as it is bigger than s^2. As the use of s'^2 is high, practically it is called the sample variance. This is the major reason why several textbooks, as well as authors, use $s^2 = \dfrac{1}{n-1}\sum_{1}^{n}\left(x_i - \bar{x}\right)^2$ as the sample variance. As slightly overestimating the variance is beneficial, this is widely accepted. The sample mean and the sample variance are respectively the point estimators for μ and σ.

Practically, several samples (random or non-random) are possible for a given population. For a clear understanding, let the population size be N for which a sample of size n is considered. There are N^n and ^NC_n possible samples depending upon whether the sampling is done with replacement or without replacement. To make it simple, consider a population having three observations 3, 5 and 7. The interest is to take a sample size of 2. That is N=3 and n=2. In the case of without replacement, all possible samples of size 2 are (3,5), (3,7) and (5,7). In the case of with replacement (the unit drawn in the previous draw is replaced before the next draw), all possible samples of size 2 are (3,5), (5,3), (3,7), (7,3), (5,7), (7,5), (3,3), (5,5) and (7,7). Thus, we see there are three possible samples that are $^3C_2$ in the case of without replacement, and nine possible samples that are 3^2 in the case of with replacement. In the without replacement case, there are three possible samples and therefore a simple random sampling has a probability of 1/3 of selecting each of these three samples. In the with replacement case, there are nine possible samples and therefore a simple random sampling has a probability of 1/9 of selecting each of these three samples. The sample means of the possible samples under the without replacement case are (4), (5) and (6), and the sample means of the possible samples under the with replacement case are (4), (4), (5), (5), (6), (6), (3), (5) and (7). The population $\mu=(3+5+7)/3=5$. The mean of the sample means under the without replacement is (4+5+6)/3=5. Also, the mean of the sample means under the with replacement is (4+4+5+5+6+6+3+5+7)/9=5. The mean of the sample means (E$\bar{x}$) equals the population mean in both with replacement and without replacement cases.

It is easy to visualize each possible sample providing a sample mean and sample variance. Sample to sample these values may differ. If random sampling is used there is a definite probability of selection for every possible sample being selected as a sample. As a result, the sample mean and variance are random variables with their own probability distributions. The probability distribution of a sample statistic created when samples of size n are repeatedly obtained from a population is known as a sampling distribution. The distribution is the sampling distribution of sample means if the sample statistic is the sample mean. The data from the sample is used to calculate the value of a sample statistic that acts as an estimate of a population parameter in point estimation.

The sample mean $\bar{x} = \dfrac{1}{n} \sum_{1}^{n} x_i$ is predominantly used as an estimator of the population mean $\mu = \dfrac{1}{N} \sum_{1}^{N} X_i$. The sampling distribution of the sample mean $\bar{x}$ is of interest. The sampling distribution of $\bar{x}$ is the probability distribution of all possible values of the sample mean $\bar{x}$. Expected value of $\bar{x} = E(\bar{x}) = \mu$. When the ratio of sample size n to population size N is less than 5 per cent, the distribution of x̄ is normally distributed with mean μ and variance σ^2/n assuming the distribution of the random variable X is normal with mean μ and variance σ^2. Theoretical developments demonstrate that when a sample of size greater than thirty is considered, the sampling distribution of x̄ can be approximated by a normal distribution regardless of the distribution of X in the population. The central limit theorem (CLT) says that if $x_1, x_2 . . ., x_n$ is a random sample of size n chosen from a population (finite or infinite) with mean μ and finite variance σ^2, and if x̄ is the sample mean, the limiting form of the distribution of $Z = \sqrt{n}\left(\dfrac{\bar{x}-\mu}{\sigma}\right)$ as n→∞, is the standard normal distribution. For small samples (n<30) the sampling distribution of x̄ will be normal only if the distribution of X is normal in the population.

Suppose that X takes the value 1 if the outcome is a success and 0 if the outcome is a failure. Then the sample proportion p̄ can be written as the sample mean x̄. If the experiment is repeated n times with observations $x_1, x_2, . . ., x_n$, then $\bar{p} = \bar{x} = \dfrac{1}{n}\sum_{1}^{n}x_i$. Then $E(\bar{p}) = p$ and $V(\bar{p}) = p(1-p)/n$. When $np \geq 5$ and $n(1-p) \geq 5$, the sampling distribution of p̄ can be approximated by a normal distribution. If p is closer to or equal to 0.50, sample sizes as small as 10 permit a normal approximation. If the value of p is either close to zero or one, normal approximation is valid only for large samples.

Example

About 75 per cent of the people living in a city own their houses. That is, the proportion of people having their own house is 0.75. The standard deviation of the people with their own house is p(1-p) = 0.1875. Based on a sample of 200 people, what is the probability that the proportion of people with their own house is within plus or minus 5 per cent of the actual proportion of people with their own house?

Given the proportion of people having their own house is 0.75, the standard deviation of the sample proportion $\bar{P}$ is $\sqrt{p(1-p)/n} = \sqrt{\frac{0.75(1-0.75)}{200}}$ = 0.030619. The proportion of people with their own house is within plus or minus 5 per cent of the actual proportion of people with their own house is P(0.70≤p≤0.80) = NORM.DIST(0.8,0.75,0.030619,1) - NORM.DIST(0.78,0.75,0.030619,1) = 0.897525.

Interval estimation

The point estimator provides a single value based on a sample drawn from the population. As the estimate is based on a single sample, the point estimator provides little information about the actual value of the population parameter. Information provided by the sample differs from sample to sample and hence the accuracy of the estimate is questionable. This poses a psychological disadvantage in addition to inaccurate estimation. The efficacy of point estimators is often understood by a probability statement based on the sampling distribution of the estimator.

An interval or range of values assumed to include the unknown population parameter is an alternative to point estimators. A measure (probability) of the confidence that the interval contains the parameter of interest is associated with the interval. This removes the bias and psychological disadvantage of using a point estimator. Interval estimation is a more robust and practical approach than point estimation. An interval estimator provides a range or interval of values that are expected to contain the population parameter of interest with an associated level of confidence. For this reason, the interval estimator is also known as a confidence interval. An interval estimate's goal is to provide information about how close the point estimate is to the parameter.

Adding and subtracting a margin of error (ME) from a point estimate yields an interval estimate. That is, the interval estimate is point estimate ± ME. The margin of error is shown in the figure below.

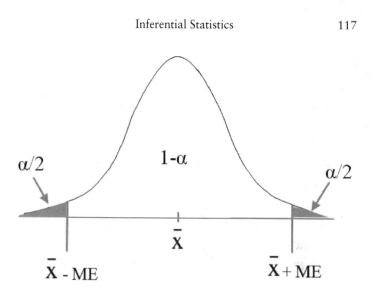

The value of ME is the value on the X-axis corresponding to the probability $\alpha/2$. The value of ME for the sampling distribution of $\bar{x}$ is $Z_{\alpha/2}\frac{\sigma}{\sqrt{n}}$. The value of $Z\alpha_{/2}$ can be computed using the Excel code NORM.S.INV(1-α/2). For example, when α=0.05, α/2=0.025, the value $Z\alpha_{/2}$ = NORM.S.INV(0.975) = 1.959963985 $\approx$ 1.96.

The interval estimate of a population mean is $\bar{x}$ $\pm$ ME. The ME can be computed using the Excel code CONFIDENCE.NORM(α,S.D,n). For proportions, instead of $\bar{x}$, $\bar{p}$ can be used. The confidence interval is ($\bar{x}$-ME, $\bar{x}$+ME). The probability that this interval is expected to include the population mean , is (1-α). This confidence interval is known as the (1-α) per cent confidence interval and the probability (1-α) is the confidence coefficient.

If the population standard deviation σ is known, the same can be used to compute ME. If the population standard deviation σ is unknown, the same can be substituted by its estimate *s,* the sample standard deviation. Under controlled environments such as industrial manufacturing, a stable level of standard deviation is maintained and hence a fairly good estimate of σ is easily available. In cases when σ is not available, σ is replaced by the sample estimates.

Example

The average weight of an apple is expected to be around 240 grams. On a large farm in Shimla, a sample of 100 apples was weighed for quality assurance purposes. The sample mean weight of an apple was 237 grams with a standard deviation of 32 grams. A 95 per cent confidence interval of the weight of the apples is found as 237 ± ME = 237 ± CONFIDENCE.NORM(0.05,32,100) = 237 grams ± 6.271884751 grams = (230.73, 243.27) grams. The interval (230.73, 243.27) is the 95 per cent confidence interval for the weight of an apple. That is, an apple from the farm can be expected to weigh between 230 gm and 243 grams.

Example

The horticulture producers cooperative marketing society (HOPCOMS) pays farmers for 80 per cent of the tomatoes procured considering about 20 per cent spoilage during transportation to their retail outlets. A sample of 30 kilograms of tomatoes in a retail outlet showed that 24.6 kilograms of tomatoes were in good condition. Is the payment by HOPCOMS justified based on a 95 per cent confidence interval?

The proportion of tomatoes HOPCOMS pays for is 0.80. This gives a standard error of

$$\sqrt{p(1-p)/n} = \sqrt{\frac{0.80(1-0,80)}{30}} = 0.073.$$ The sample

proportion of tomatoes that were in good condition is 24.6/30 = 0.82. Based on the payments by HOPCPMS, the 95 per cent confidence interval for the proportion of tomatoes in good condition is 0.80 ± ME. That is 0.80 ± CONFIDENCE.NORM(0.05,0.073029674,30) = 0.80 ± 0.026 = (0.774, 0.826). The sample proportion of tomatoes that were found in good condition was 0.82, which is included in this confidence interval. Hence it may be concluded that the payment by HOPCOMS is justified.

Interval estimation for small samples

When the population standard deviation is unknown and the sample size is less than thirty, it is not recommended to use the normal approximation for the distribution of the sample mean. The confidence intervals are calculated using the student t-distribution if the distribution of X in the population can be considered to be symmetric. When the population standard deviation is unknown and the data come from a normally distributed population, the t-distribution characterizes the normalized distances between sample means and the population mean. The t-distribution was originally described by William Sealy Gosset (1876–1937) who pioneered small sample experimental design and analysis. His research works were published under his pseudonym 'student' and hence the name student t-distribution. In the case of unknown σ^2 and n < 30, the margin of error (ME) in the interval estimator for the population mean $\bar{x} \pm ME$ is obtained using the Excel code CONFIDENCE.T(α, S.D,n). The value of ME for the sampling distribution of $\bar{x}$ when n<30 based on t-distribution is $t\alpha_{/2} \dfrac{s}{\sqrt{n}}$. The value of $t\alpha_{/2}$ can be computed using the Excel code T.INV(1-α/2,d.f) where the degrees of freedom (d.f) is (n-1). For example, when α=0.05, α/2=0.025, n=25, the value $t\alpha_{/2}$ = T.INV(0.975,24) = 2.063898562 $\approx$ 2.06.

Example

A sample of eighteen rentable independent houses in a posh area close to the business district of a city provides an average monthly rental of Rs 40,000 and a standard deviation of Rs 8000. The 95 per cent confidence interval estimate of the average rent per month for independent houses around the business district is 40000±CONFIDENCE.T(0.05,8000,18) = 40000 ± 3978.31= (36,021.69, 43,978.31).

Example

A doctor at the All India Institute of Medical Sciences (AIIMS) wished to estimate the mean blood sugar level for all adult men living in Delhi and affected by the COVID-19 virus. He took a sample of twenty-five adult men from Delhi who had contracted COVID-19 and found that the mean blood sugar level in this sample was 136 with a standard deviation of twenty-six. Assuming that the blood sugar level for all adult men in Delhi who had contracted COVID-19 is approximately normally distributed, the 99 per cent confidence interval for the mean blood sugar level of adult men affected by COVID-19 is 136±CONFIDENCE.T(0.01,26,25) = 136 ± 14.54408542 = (121.4559146, 150.5440854).

In practical business situations, there have been continuous discussions on random and non-random samples and unbiased and biased estimates. Today, the random sample itself is in question as most of the time samples from online surveys, electronic surveys and social media are used. Other than in scientifically designed experiments, industrial quality control inspections, etc., random samples are seldom used. Even in sophisticated manufacturing processes like bread (maximizing the volume of bread for given inputs), wine and beer (getting the desired colour and aroma) etc., the use of biased estimates may be seen as the closeness to the expected parameter values is considered more important than satisfying a mathematical property like unbiasedness. This is more prevalent in chemometric applications. Customer satisfaction supersedes mathematical properties.

Hypotheses and testing of hypotheses

A hypothesis is a statement or an assertion or a claim or an assumption about an unknown population parameter the validity of which can be tested. For example, *the accused is innocent* and $\mu=100$ are hypotheses. Every hypothesis implies its contradiction or alternative. For example, *the accused is guilty* and $\mu \neq 100$. A hypothesis is either true or false. In practice, a hypothesis may be rejected or failed to be rejected based on the information obtained from the sample.

Null and alternative hypotheses

The null hypothesis indicated by H_0 is a hypothesis that can be proved false based on observed data. By definition, the null hypothesis is a statement of zero or no change and often represents the status quo situation or an existing belief. The null hypothesis is always written with the equality sign $\leq$ or $=$ or $\geq$. A hypothesis written with one of the signs $<$, or $\neq$, or > is the complement of the null hypothesis. The null hypothesis has the right of equality sign. An alternative hypothesis is a statement that is true if the null hypothesis is false. The test for testing the validity of the hypothesis is called one-sided (one-tailed) if the sign of the alternative hypothesis is < or > and two-sided (two-tailed) if the sign of the alternative hypothesis is =. The null and alternative hypotheses are mutually exclusive. That is, only one of the two can be true.

A hypothesis is assumed true until a decision is made to reject it as false or not to reject it as true. Because the decision to reject or not to reject a hypothesis is based on the evidence produced by the sample information, a true hypothesis may be falsely rejected or a false hypothesis may not be rejected. A decision to reject or fail to reject a hypothesis may be correct if a true hypothesis is not rejected. Similarly, a decision to reject or fail to reject a hypothesis may be incorrect if a true hypothesis is rejected or a false hypothesis is not rejected. A decision may be correct in two ways, i.e., fail to reject a true H_0 and reject a false H_0. A decision may be incorrect in two ways, i.e., reject a true H_0 (type I error) and fail to reject a false H_0 (type II error).

Decision	H_0 is true	H_0 is false
Reject H_0	Type I error	Correct decision
Fail to reject H_0	Correct decision	Type II error

Until recently, the testing of hypotheses was based on the two types of errors and the probabilities of committing such errors. While it was not clear whether type I or type II was more serious in practice, test procedures were developed by assuming a very small probability for the type I error and minimizing the probability of the type II error. The assumed small value of the probability of a type I error was denoted by α and was called the level of significance. The resulting probability of a type II error was denoted by β and the complement of the probability of the type II error $(1-\beta)$ was called the power of the test. In the recent past, these concepts have become obsolete.

Testing for the population mean

In most business scenarios and practical situations, the estimate of the population mean is often of interest. An assumption about the population mean is made, and the validity of such an assumption being true is tested using a sample taken from the population. The sample is taken from a normal or near-normal population so that the sampling distribution is symmetric and unimodal. There are three sets of hypotheses possible for testing for the population mean when the population variance σ^2 is known as well as unknown. When the distribution of the random variable under consideration is normal or the sample size $n \geq 30$, the testing for the population mean is based on the normal distribution. When $n \geq 30$ and σ^2 is unknown, the estimate s^2 of σ^2 is used.

When the distribution of the random variable under consideration is normal or near-normal and the sample size n < 30, the testing for the population mean is based on the t-distribution.

The null and alternative hypotheses about a population mean in general may take any one of the following three possibilities:

(a) H_0: $\mu \geq \mu_0$; H_1: $\mu < \mu_0$
(b) H_0: $\mu \leq \mu_0$; H_1: $\mu > \mu_0$, and
(c) H_0: $\mu = \mu_0$; H_1: $\mu \neq \mu_0$

where μ_0 is the hypothesized value of μ. The alternative hypotheses can take *only* any one of the signs <, ≠, and >, based on which the hypotheses are recognized as one-tailed or two-tailed (one-sided or two-sided). The null hypotheses are the complements of the alternative hypotheses. In practice, the hypothesis that needs to be proved or established is considered the alternative hypothesis. Based on the alternative hypotheses, the critical and noncritical regions for the null hypotheses to be true are decided. The probability that is permissible for the sample mean to exceed the margin of error is usually denoted by α. The value of α is fixed as small as possible depending on the requirements of the practitioner, like α=0.05 or 0.01. In case no value α is prescribed, the default value of α=0.05 is used. If based on the sample results, the actual probability to exceed the margin of error is less than the pre-decided α the null hypothesis is rejected.

The critical regions for the three possible alternative hypotheses are explained in the following figure.

Testing for the population mean with known variance

Assume that the population size is N with mean μ and known variance σ^2. A sample is taken from the population with size n and its sample mean $\bar{x}$ is obtained. If the characteristic of interest (measured by the random variable X) follows a normal distribution in the population with mean μ and variance σ^2, then the sample mean $\bar{x}$ is also normally distributed with mean μ and variance σ^2/n.

There are three possible sets of hypotheses, as given below.

(a). $H_0: \mu \leq \mu_0$; $H_1: \mu > \mu_0$

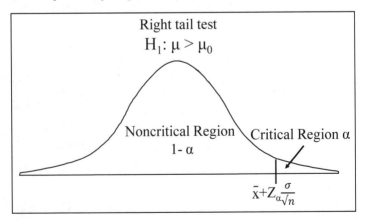

Right tail test
$H_1: \mu > \mu_0$

Noncritical Region
$1 - \alpha$

Critical Region α

$\bar{x} + Z_\alpha \dfrac{\sigma}{\sqrt{n}}$

To test this hypothesis, find the $P(\bar{x} > \mu_0)$ using the Excel code 1-NORM.DIST($\bar{x}$,μ_0,S.D,1). S.D is the standard deviation of the sample mean $(\frac{\sigma}{\sqrt{n}})$. If this probability is $\leq \alpha$, the desired value for the probability that $\bar{x}$ exceeds the margin of error, reject the null hypothesis. Or else, do not reject the null hypothesis.

Example

A patient has to wait on an average twenty minutes with a standard deviation of six minutes to meet a specialist doctor in a reputed hospital. A random sample of thirty-six patients showed a mean waiting time of 22.5 minutes. Does the sample result evidence the claim of the hospital concerning the average waiting time?

The null and alternative hypotheses are:

H_0: $\mu \leq 20$ minutes; H_1: $\mu > 20$ minutes.

The $P(\bar{x} > 20)$ using the Excel code 1-NORM.DIST $(\bar{x},\mu_0,S.D,1) = 1\text{-}NORM.DIST(22.5,20,6/6,1) = 0.0062097 < 0.05$ (α). Hence, the null hypothesis is rejected. The sample results do not support the claim of the hospital that the average waiting time for a patient is twenty minutes.

(b). $H_0: \mu \geq \mu_0$; $H_1: \mu < \mu_0$

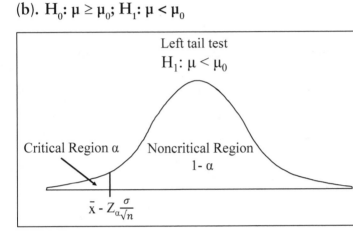

To test this hypothesis, find the $P(\bar{x} < \mu_0)$ using the Excel code NORM.DIST($\bar{x}, \mu_0$, S.D, 1). S.D is the standard deviation of the sample mean $(\frac{\sigma}{\sqrt{n}})$. If this probability is $\leq \alpha$, the desired value for the probability that $\bar{x}$ falls below the margin of error, reject the null hypothesis. Or else, do not reject the null hypothesis.

Example

An ayurvedic syrup is sold in bottles of 300 ml. As the syrup is filled manually, the quantity of the syrup filled in the bottles follows a normal distribution with a known standard deviation of forty ml. A random sample of sixty bottles showed a mean of 280 ml. Does the sample show that the filling process is under-filling?

The null and alternative hypotheses are:

H_0: $\mu \geq 300$ ml; H_1: $\mu < 300$ ml.

The $P(\bar{x}<300)$ using the Excel code NORM.DIST $(\bar{x},\mu_0,S.D,1)$ = NORM.DIST$(280,300,40/\sqrt{60},1)$ = NORM.DIST$(280,300,5.163977795,1)$ = 0.00005376 < 0.05 (α). Hence, the null hypothesis is rejected, and it is concluded that the sample results evidence that the filling process is under-filling.

(c). H_0: $\mu = \mu_0$; H_1: $\mu \neq \mu_0$

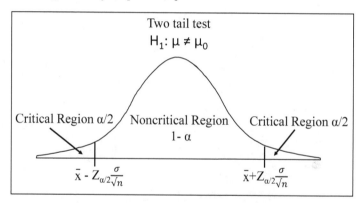

To test this hypothesis, find either the $P(\bar{x}<\mu_0)$ using the Excel code NORM.DIST$(\bar{x},\mu_0,S.D,1)$ or $P(\bar{x}>\mu_0)$ using the Excel code 1-NORM.DIST$(\bar{x},\mu_0,S.D,1)$. S.D is the standard deviation of the sample mean $(\frac{\sigma}{\sqrt{n}})$. If either of these probabilities is $\leq \alpha/2$, the desired value for the probability that $\bar{x}$ falls below the margin of error or falls above the margin of error, reject the null hypothesis. Or else, do not reject the null hypothesis.

Example

A newly invented engine is expected to run continuously for ninety minutes per litre of fuel with a proven standard deviation of twenty minutes. Suppose a simple random sample of fifty engines tested provided an average of ninety-five minutes of continuous running, can it be concluded that the claim about the newly developed engine is met?

The null and alternative hypotheses are:

H_0: μ = 95 minutes; H_1: $\mu \neq 95$ minutes.

Since $\bar{x}-\mu_0$ = 95-90 is > 0, find $P(\bar{x}>\mu_0)$ using the Excel code 1-NORM.DIST($\bar{x},\mu_0$,S.D,1) where S.D is the standard deviation of the sample mean ($\frac{\sigma}{\sqrt{n}}$). Reject the null hypothesis if $P(\bar{x}>\mu_0) \leq 0.025$ ($\alpha/2$). Here, 1-NORM.DIST($\bar{x},\mu_0$,S.D,1) = 1-NORM.DIST(95,90,20/$\sqrt{50}$,1) = 0.0385499 > 0.025. Hence, the null hypothesis is not rejected, and it is concluded that the claim about the newly developed engine is met.

Testing for the population mean with unknown variance

Assume that the population size is N with mean μ and unknown variance σ^2. A sample is taken from the population with size n and its sample mean $\bar{x}$ and the sample variance $s^2 = \dfrac{1}{n-1}\sum_1^n\left(x_i - \bar{x}\right)^2$ are obtained. If the characteristic of interest (measured by the random variable X) follows a normal distribution in the population with mean μ and variance σ^2, then the sample mean $\bar{x}$ is also normally distributed with mean μ and variance σ^2/n. As σ^2 is unknown, the same is replaced by its estimator s^2. If the distribution of X is unknown, then $\bar{x}$ will be asymptotically normally distributed when $n \geq 30$. If σ^2 is unknown, then the same is replaced by its estimator s^2.

There are three possible sets of hypotheses, as given below.

(a). $H_0: \mu \leq \mu_0$; $H_1: \mu > \mu_0$

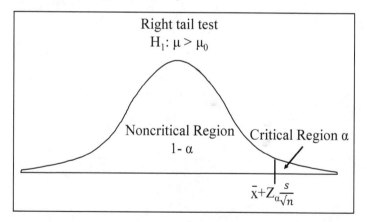

To test this hypothesis, find the $P(\bar{x} > \mu_0)$ using the Excel code $1 - NORM.DIST(\bar{x}, \mu_0, S.D, 1)$. S.D is the standard deviation of the sample mean $(\frac{s}{\sqrt{n}})$. If this probability is $\leq \alpha$, the desired value for the probability that $\bar{x}$ exceeding the margin of error, reject the null hypothesis. Or else, do not reject the null hypothesis.

Example

The average weight of adults in the age group twenty-one to twenty-five years is expected to be sixty-eight kg. A random sample of sixty-four students of a business school showed a mean weight of seventy-one kg with a standard deviation of 10 kg. Does the sample result show that the students of the business school are overweight?

The null and alternative hypotheses are:

$H_0: \mu \le 68$ kg; $H_1: \mu > 68$ kg.

The $P(\bar{x} > 68)$ using the Excel code 1-NORM.DIST($\bar{x}, \mu_0, S.D, 1$) = 1- NORM.DIST(71,68,10/$\sqrt{64}$,1) = 0.00819754 < 0.05 (α). Hence, the null hypothesis is rejected. The sample results show that the students of the business school are overweight.

(b). $H_0: \mu \ge \mu_0$; $H_1: \mu < \mu_0$

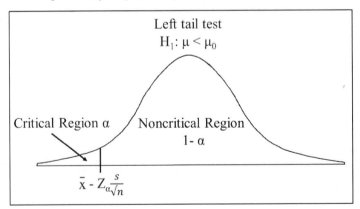

To test this hypothesis, find the $P(\bar{x}<\mu_0)$ using the Excel code NORM.DIST($\bar{x}$,μ_0,S.D,1). S.D is the standard deviation of the sample mean ($\frac{s}{\sqrt{n}}$). If this probability is $\leq \alpha$, the desired value for the probability that $\bar{x}$ falls below the margin of error, reject the null hypothesis. Or else, do not reject the null hypothesis.

Example

A smart school in a city claims that the average IQ of its students is at least 110. To check this claim, a random sample of thirty-six students was taken and the students were administered an IQ test. The average score of the students was 108 with a standard deviation of seven. Do the sample results support the claim of the school?

The null and alternative hypotheses are:

H_0: $\mu \geq 110$; H_1: $\mu < 110$.

The $P(\bar{x}<110)$ using the Excel code NORM.DIST ($\bar{x}$,μ_0,S.D,1) = NORM.DIST(108,110,7/$\sqrt{36}$,1) = 0.043238 < 0.05 (α). Hence, the null hypothesis is rejected, and it is concluded that the sample results do not support the claim of the school.

H_0: $\mu = \mu_0$; H_1: $\mu \neq \mu_0$

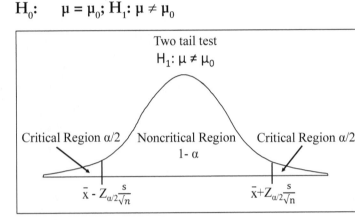

To test this hypothesis, find either the $P(\bar{x}<\mu_0)$ using the Excel code NORM.DIST($\bar{x}$,μ_0,S.D,1) or $P(\bar{x}>\mu_0)$ using the Excel code 1-NORM.DIST($\bar{x}$,μ_0,S.D,1). S.D is the standard deviation of the sample mean ($\frac{s}{\sqrt{n}}$). If either of these probabilities is $\leq \alpha/2$, the desired value for the probability that $\bar{x}$ falls below the margin of error or falls above the margin of error, reject the null hypothesis. Or else, do not reject the null hypothesis.

Example

The manufactured net weight of a branded bar of soap is 125 grams. Suspecting this to be true, a random sample of 100 soap bars was tested, and it was found that the average weight of the soaps in the sample was 123.5 grams with a standard deviation of five grams.

Based on the sample results can it be concluded that the manufactured net weight of the soap bar is 125 grams?

The null and alternative hypotheses are:

H_0: μ = 125 grams; H_1: $\mu \neq$ 125 grams.

Since $\bar{x}-\mu_0$ = 123.5-125 is < 0, find $P(\bar{x}<\mu_0)$ using the Excel code NORM.DIST($\bar{x},\mu_0$,S.D,1) where S.D is the standard deviation of the sample mean ($\frac{s}{\sqrt{n}}$). Reject the null hypothesis if $P(\bar{x}<\mu_0) \leq 0.025$ (α/2). Here, NORM.DIST($\bar{x},\mu_0$,S.D,1) = NORM.DIST(123.5,125,5/$\sqrt{100}$,1) = 0.0013499 < 0.025. Hence, the null hypothesis is rejected, and it is concluded that the manufactured net weight of the soap bar is not 125 grams.

Testing for the population mean with unknown variance using a t-test

Assume that in a population of size N, the characteristic of interest (measured by the random variable X) is assumed to follow a normal distribution with mean μ and unknown variance σ^2. A small sample (n<30) is taken from the population with size n, and its sample mean $\bar{x}$ and the sample variance $s^2 = \frac{1}{n-1}\sum_{1}^{n}\left(x_i - \bar{x}\right)^2$ are obtained.

There are three possible sets of hypotheses, as given below.

(a). $H_0: \mu \le \mu_0$; $H_1: \mu > \mu_0$

Right tail test
$H_1: \mu > \mu_0$

Noncritical Region
$1 - \alpha$

Critical Region α

$\bar{x} + t_\alpha \dfrac{s}{\sqrt{n}}$

To test this hypothesis, find the $P(\bar{x} > \mu_0)$ using the Excel code $1 - \text{T.DIST}((\bar{x} - \mu_0)/\text{SD}, n-1, 1)$ where $SD = \dfrac{s}{\sqrt{n}}$. If this probability is $\le \alpha$, the desired value for the probability that $\bar{x}$ exceeds the margin of error, reject the null hypothesis. Or else, do not reject the null hypothesis.

Example

A motorcycle manufacturing company claims that their newly introduced 100 cc motorcycle gives a mileage of sixty kilometres per litre of petrol. A sample test ride of twenty-five motorcycles provided an average of 61.2 kilometres with a standard deviation of 3.1 kilometres per litre of petrol. Is there evidence that the average mileage exceeded the claim of the company?

The null and alternative hypotheses are:

$H_0: \mu \le 60; H_1: \mu > 60$

Given, $\bar{x} = 61.2$, SD $= \dfrac{s}{\sqrt{n}} = 3.1/\sqrt{25} = 0.62$, the $P(\bar{x} > 60)$ using the Excel code 1- T.DIST($(\bar{x}-\mu_0)$/SD,n-1,1) = 1-T.DIST(1.2/0.62,24,1) = 0.032398896 < 0.05 (α). Hence, the null hypothesis is rejected. There is evidence that the average mileage exceeded the claim of the company.

(b). $H_0: \mu \ge \mu_0; H_1: \mu < \mu_0$

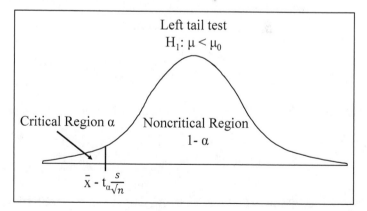

To test this hypothesis, find the $P(\bar{x}<\mu_0)$ using the Excel code T.DIST$((\bar{x}-\mu_0)/SD, n-1,1)$ S.D is the standard deviation of the sample mean $(\frac{s}{\sqrt{n}})$. If this probability is $\leq \alpha$, the desired value for the probability that $\bar{x}$ falls below the margin of error, reject the null hypothesis. Or else, do not reject the null hypothesis.

Example

A leading car manufacturer claims that a newly introduced auto transmission car gives an average mileage of twenty-one kilometres per litre of petrol. A sample of twelve cars was test-driven. The test drive resulted in an average mileage of nineteen kilometres per litre of petrol with a standard deviation of three kilometres. Do the sample results support the claim of the manufacturer?

The null and alternative hypotheses are:

H_0: $\mu \geq 21$; H_1: $\mu < 21$.

Given, $\bar{x} = 19$, SD $= \frac{s}{\sqrt{n}} = 3/\sqrt{12} = 0.866025$, the P($\bar{x}<21$) using the Excel code T.DIST$((\bar{x}-\mu_0)/SD,n-1,1)$ = T.DIST$(-2/0.866025,12-1,1)$ = $0.020671 < 0.05$ (α). Hence, the null hypothesis is rejected, and it is concluded that the sample results do not support the claim of the car manufacturer.

(c). $H_0: \mu = \mu_0$; $H_1: \mu \neq \mu_0$

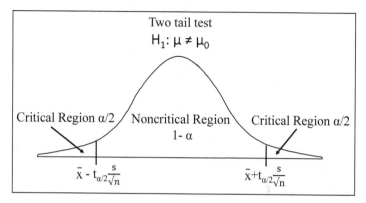

To test this hypothesis, find either the $P(\bar{x} < \mu_0)$ using the Excel code T.DIST($(\bar{x}-\mu_0)$/SD,n-1,1) or $P(\bar{x} > \mu_0)$ using the Excel code 1-T.DIST($(\bar{x}-\mu_0)$/SD,n-1,1) where S.D is the standard deviation of the sample mean $(\frac{s}{\sqrt{n}})$.

If either of these probabilities is $\leq \alpha/2$, the desired value for the probability that $\bar{x}$ falls below the margin of error or falls above the margin of error, reject the null hypothesis. Or else, do not reject the null hypothesis.

Example

The historical data of an insurance company INSCo shows that the average age of people who buy their first life insurance plan is thirty-five years. A random sample of fifteen customers who had just purchased their first life insurance policy showed their average

age was 32.5 years with a standard deviation of six years. Can it be concluded that these customers have purchased the insurance from INSCo?

H_0: μ = 35 years; H_1: $\mu \neq$ 35 years.

Since $\bar{x}-\mu_0$ = 32.5-35 is < 0, find $P(\bar{x}<\mu_0)$ using the Excel code T.DIST($(\bar{x}-\mu_0)$/SD,n-1,1) where S.D is the standard deviation of the sample mean ($\frac{s}{\sqrt{n}}$). Reject the null hypothesis if $P(\bar{x}<\mu_0) \leq 0.025$ ($\alpha/2$). Here, T.DIST(($\bar{x}-\mu_0$)/SD,n-1,1) = T.DIST((32.5-35)/(6/$\sqrt{15}$),15-1,1) = T.DIST(-2.5/1.549193,14,1) = 0.064445 > 0.025. Hence, the null hypothesis is not rejected, and it is concluded that the average age of the customers who buy their first life insurance plan is thiryt-five years. It may be concluded that these customers have purchased the insurance from INSCo.

Testing for the population proportion

A portion or part of the population is known as a proportion. Imagine a binomial situation where X represents the total number of successes out of N trials. Then the proportion of successes p = $\frac{X}{N}$. Then the V(p)= $\frac{p(1-p)}{N}$. When p is unknown a sample of n units is taken from the population of N units, and let x be the number of successes found in the sample of n units. Then the sample proportion is $\bar{p} = \frac{x}{n}$, and the variance of $\bar{p}$ is V($\bar{p}$) = $\frac{\bar{p}(1-\bar{p})}{n}$. The hypotheses for the population proportion p are as under. The general forms of null and alternative hypotheses are

(a) $H_0: p \leq p_0$; $H_1: p > p_0$
(b) $H_0: p \geq p_0$; $H_1: p < p_0$
(c) $H_0: p = p_0$; $H_1: p \neq p_0$

where p_0 is the hypothesized value of the population proportion p. The test procedure is based on the assumption of normal distribution under the conditions that $np \geq 5$ and $n(1-p) \geq 5$.

(a). $H_0: p \leq p_0$; $H_1: p > p_0$

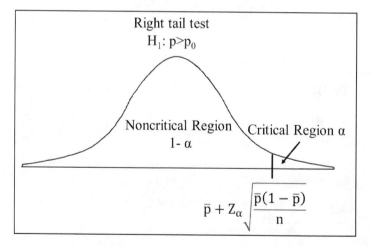

To test the above hypotheses, find the $P(\bar{p} > p_0)$ using the Excel code 1-NORM.DIST$(\bar{p}, p_0, \sqrt{\frac{\bar{p}(1-\bar{p})}{n}}, 1)$.

If $P(\bar{p} > p_0) \leq \alpha$, the desired value for the probability that $\bar{p}$ falls below the margin of error, reject the null hypothesis. Or else, do not reject the null hypothesis.

Example

In an assembly meeting, it was decided to resolve an issue by voting. It was expected that more than 60 per cent of the members present would vote in favour of the issue. Out of the 250 members considered in a random sample, 180 voted in favour of the issue. Does the sample show the expectation of the voting?

The hypotheses are H_0: $p \leq 0.60$; H_1: $p > 0.60$.

Here $\bar{p}$ = 180/250 = 0.72 and $V(\bar{p}) = \sqrt{\frac{0.72(1-0.72)}{250}}$ = 0.028397.

The probability $P(\bar{p} > 0.60)$ using the Excel code $1 - \text{NORM.DIST}(\bar{p}, p_0, \sqrt{\frac{\bar{p}(1-\bar{p})}{n}}, 1)$ = 1- NORM.DIST(0.72,0.60,0.028397,1) = 0.00001190. The $P(\bar{p} > 0.60) < 0.05$ (α) the null hypothesis is rejected and concluded in favour of the alternative hypothesis. The sample results justified the expectation of the proportion of members voting in favour of the issue.

(b). H_0: $p \geq p_0$; H_1: $p < p_0$

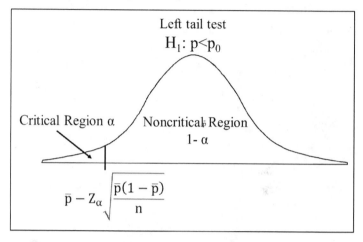

To test this hypothesis, find the $P(\bar{p}<p_0)$ using the Excel code NORM.DIST($\bar{p}$,p_0,$\sqrt{\frac{p(1-\bar{p})}{n}}$,1)). If $P(\bar{p}<p_0)$ $\leq \alpha$, the desired value for the probability that $\bar{p}$ falls below the margin of error, reject the null hypothesis. Or else, do not reject the null hypothesis.

Example

A manufacturer of resistors used in microwave appliances has to guarantee that the proportion of defective resistors is under 5 per cent. A microwave oven manufacturer desiring to check the process capability of the manufacturer of the resistors inspected a sample of 200 resistors at random and observed that there were four defective resistors. Based on the sample information, can the manufacturer of resistors showcase the process capability?

The hypotheses are H_0: $p \geq 0.05$; H_1: $p < 0.05$.

Given the sample information, $\bar{p} = 4/200 = 0.02$ and the standard deviation of $\bar{p}$ is $\frac{\sqrt{(0.02)(0.98)}}{\sqrt{200}}$ = 0.009899495. Hence, $P(\bar{p} < 0.05)$ = NORM.DIST(0.02,0.05,0.009899495,1)=0.001220917. Since $P(\bar{p} < 0.05) < 0.05$ (α), the null hypothesis is rejected. The manufacturer of the resistors can showcase the process capability.

(c). H_0: $p = p_0$; H_1: $p \neq p_0$

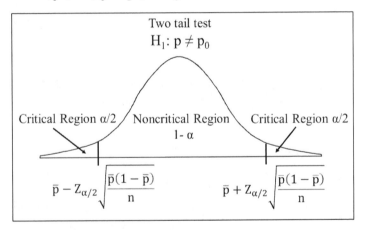

To test this hypothesis, find either the $P(\bar{p}<p_0)$ using the Excel code $\text{NORM.DIST}(\bar{p},p_0,\sqrt{\frac{\bar{p}(1-\bar{p})}{n}},1)$ or $P(\bar{p}>p_0)$ using the Excel code $1-\text{NORM.DIST}(\bar{p},p_0,\sqrt{\frac{\bar{p}(1-\bar{p})}{n}},1)$. If either of $P(\bar{p}<p_0)$ and $P(\bar{p}>p_0)$ is $\leq \alpha/2$, the desired value for the probability that $\bar{p}$ falls below the margin of error or falls above the margin of error, reject the null hypothesis. Or else, do not reject the null hypothesis.

Example

A biotech company that manufactures antivirus vaccines claimed that about 15 per cent of the people vaccinated may experience a stupor. In a vaccination campaign of this antivirus, eighty-one of the 900 people vaccinated experienced a stupor. Is the claim of the biotech company justified?

The hypotheses are H_0: $p = 0.10$; H_1: $p \neq 0.10$.

Given the information $p_0=0.10$, $\bar{p}=81/900=0.09$ and the standard deviation of $\bar{p}$ is $\frac{\sqrt{(0.09)(0.91)}}{\sqrt{900}}$ = 0.009539. $P(\bar{p}<0.10)$ = $\text{NORM.DIST}(0.09,0.10,0.009539,1)$ = 0.147244. Since $P(\bar{p}<0.10) > 0.05$ (α), the null hypothesis is not rejected and it is concluded that the claim of the pharma company is justified.

Two populations

Let there be two populations. Consider a manufacturing company that has two plants in two different cities, manufacturing the same product with the same specifications. It would be of interest to know if these two manufacturing plants make identical products. It is reasonable to believe make zbased on the history of the plants that the variance of the quality characteristic variables is maintained (controlled) to an acceptable low value and therefore known. To test if the manufactured products are identical, the hypothesis that the means of the two populations (the means in the two plants) are the same is tested.

Two populations with known equal variance

Assume that the two populations are of size N_1 and N_2 with means μ_1 and μ_2 with known equal variances $\sigma_1^2 = \sigma_2^2 = \sigma^2$. Assume two samples are taken from these two populations with sizes n_1 and n_2 and their sample means $\bar{x}_1$ and $\bar{x}_2$ are obtained. If the characteristic of interest (measured by the random variable X) follows a normal distribution in the population with mean μ and variance σ^2, then the difference of the sample means $(\bar{x}_1 - \bar{x}_2)$ is also normally distributed with mean $\mu_1 - \mu_2$ and variance $\sigma^2 \left(\frac{1}{n_1} + \frac{1}{n_2} \right)$.

Population 1 Size N_1 Mean $= \mu_1$ Variance $= \sigma^2$ Sample mean $= \bar{x}_1$	Population 2 Size N_2 Mean $= \mu_2$ Variance $= \sigma^2$ Sample mean $= \bar{x}_2$

There are usually three possible sets of hypotheses:

(a). $H_0: \mu_1 = \mu_2$ (or) $H_0: \mu_1 . \mu_2 = 0$

$H_1: \mu_1 \neq \mu_2$ (or) $H_1: \mu_1 - \mu_2 \neq 0$

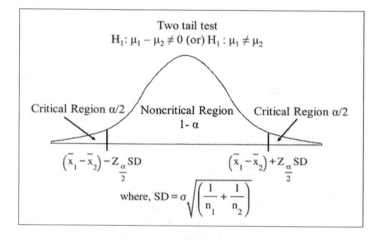

Find $\{P(\bar{x}_1 - \bar{x}_2) < 0\}$ if $(\bar{x}_1 - \bar{x}_2) < 0$ using the Excel code NORM.DIST$((\bar{x}_1 - \bar{x}_2), 0, \sigma\sqrt{\frac{1}{n_1} + \frac{1}{n_2}}, 1)$ or find $\{P(\bar{x}_1 - \bar{x}_2) > 0\}$ if $(\bar{x}_1 - \bar{x}_2) > 0$ using the Excel code 1-NORM.DIST$((\bar{x}_1 - \bar{x}_2), 0, \sigma\sqrt{\frac{1}{n_1} + \frac{1}{n_2}}, 1)$. If either of these probabilities is $\leq \alpha/2$, the desired value for the probability that $(\bar{x}_1 - \bar{x}_2)$ falls below the margin of error or falls above the margin of error, the null hypothesis is rejected. Or else, the null hypothesis is not rejected.

(b). H$_0$: μ$_1$ ≥ μ$_2$ (or) H$_0$: μ$_1$.μ$_2$ ≥ 0

H$_1$: μ$_1$ < μ$_2$ (or) H$_1$: μ$_1$-μ$_2$ < 0

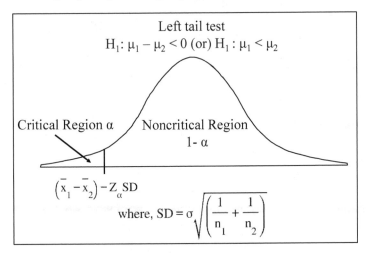

Find $\{P(\bar{x}_1-\bar{x}_2) < 0\}$ using the Excel code NORM. DIST($(\bar{x}_1-\bar{x}_2)$,0,$\sigma\sqrt{\frac{1}{n_1}+\frac{1}{n_2}}$,1). If $\{P(\bar{x}_1-\bar{x}_2) < 0\}$ is less than α, the null hypothesis is rejected. Or else, the null hypothesis is not rejected.

(c). H_0: $\mu_1 \leq \mu_2$ (or) H_0: $\mu_1 . \mu_2 \leq 0$

H_1: $\mu_1 > \mu_2$ (or) H_1: $\mu_1 - \mu_2 > 0$

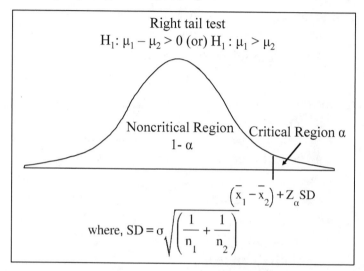

Find $1 - \{P(\bar{x}_1 - \bar{x}_2) > 0\}$ using the Excel code 1-NORM. DIST($(\bar{x}_1 - \bar{x}_2), 0, \sigma\sqrt{\frac{1}{n_1} + \frac{1}{n_2}}, 1$). If $1 - \{P(\bar{x}_1 - \bar{x}_2) > 0\}$ is less than α, the null hypothesis is rejected. Or else, the null hypothesis is not rejected.

Example

A manufacturer of enamel paints attempted to add a drying agent to reduce the drying time of a primer brand. The history of the plant shows the standard deviation of drying time is eight minutes. One sample of thirty specimens of the regular paint and another sample of thirty-five specimens of the paint with added drying agent were tested in random order. The sample average drying times of these two paints were 121 minutes and 115 minutes respectively. The interest here is to see if the addition of the drying agent is effective. Assume $\alpha = 0.05$.

The two hypotheses are:

H_0: The drying time of the regular paint and the drying time of the paint with added drying agent are the same.

H_1: The drying time of the regular paint and the drying time of the paint with added drying agent are not the same.

Alternatively stated:

H_0: $\mu_1 = \mu_2$ (or) H_0: $\mu_1 - \mu_2 = 0$
H_1: $\mu_1 \mu_2$ (or) H_0: $\mu_1 - \mu_2$ 0

Given the values of $\bar{x}_1 = 121$, $\bar{x}_2 = 115$, and $\sigma = 8$, the $1 - \{P(\bar{x}_1 - \bar{x}_2) > 0\}$ is found as $1 - \text{NORM.DIST}(121 - 115, 0, 8, \sqrt{\frac{1}{30} + \frac{1}{35}}, 1)$ = 0.001287489, which is less than 0,025 ($\alpha/2$). Hence hypothesis H_0 is rejected. When H_0 is rejected, the conclusion favours the alternative hypothesis H_1. That is, the average drying time of the regular paint and the paint with added drying agent are not the same.

In this case, as the manufacturer intends to reduce the drying time, the null and alternative hypotheses may be considered as:

H_0: The average drying time of the regular paint and the average drying time of the paint with added drying agent are the same.

H_1: The average drying time of the paint with an added agent is less than the average drying time of the regular paint.

Alternatively stated:

H_0: $\mu_1 \leq \mu_2$ (or) H_0: $\mu_1 - \mu_2 \leq 0$
H_1: $\mu_1 > \mu_2$ (or) H_0: $\mu_1 - \mu_2 > 0$

Accordingly, $1 - \{P(\bar{x}_1 - \bar{x}_2) > 0\} = 0.001287489$, which is less than $\alpha = 0.05$. Hence, H_0 is rejected and concluded in favour of the alternative hypothesis H_1. It may be concluded that based on the sample results, adding the drying agent to the paint reduces the average drying time.

Two populations with known unequal variances

Assume that the two populations are of size N_1 and N_2 with means μ_1 and μ_2 with known but unequal variances σ_1^2 and σ_2^2. Assume two samples are taken from these two populations with sizes n_1 and n_2 and their sample means $\bar{x}_1$ and $\bar{x}_2$ are obtained. If the characteristic of interest (measured by the random variable X) follows a normal distribution in the populations with mean μ_1 and μ_2, and variance σ_1^2 and σ_2^2, the difference of the sample means $(\bar{x}_1 - \bar{x}_2)$ will be normally distributed with a mean $(\mu_1 - \mu_2)$ and variance $\left(\frac{\sigma_1^2}{n_1} + \frac{\sigma_2^2}{n_2}\right)$.

Population 1	Population 2
Size N_1	Size N_2
Mean $= \mu_1$	Mean $= \mu_2$
Variance $= \sigma_1^2$	Variance $= \sigma_2^2$
Sample mean $= \bar{x}_1$	Sample mean $= \bar{x}_2$

There are usually three possible sets of hypotheses.

(a). H_0: $\mu_1 = \mu_2$ (or) H_0: $\mu_1 - \mu_2 = 0$

H_1: $\mu_1 \neq \mu_2$ (or) H_1: $\mu_1 - \mu_2 \neq 0$

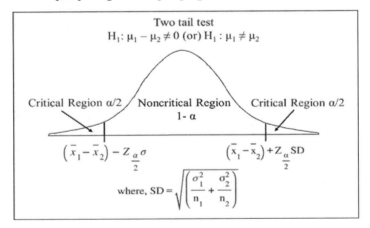

Two tail test
H_1: $\mu_1 - \mu_2 \neq 0$ (or) H_1: $\mu_1 \neq \mu_2$

Critical Region $\alpha/2$ Noncritical Region   Critical Region $\alpha/2$
1- α

$\left(\bar{x}_1 - \bar{x}_2\right) - Z_{\frac{\alpha}{2}}\sigma$ $\left(\bar{x}_1 - \bar{x}_2\right) + Z_{\frac{\alpha}{2}} SD$

where, $SD = \sqrt{\left(\frac{\sigma_1^2}{n_1} + \frac{\sigma_2^2}{n_2}\right)}$

Find $\{P(\bar{x}_1 - \bar{x}_2) < 0\}$ if $(\bar{x}_1 - \bar{x}_2) < 0$ using the Excel code NORM.DIST$((\bar{x}_1 - \bar{x}_2), 0, \sqrt{\frac{\sigma_1^2}{n_1} + \frac{\sigma_2^2}{n_2}}, 1)$ or find $\{P(\bar{x}_1 - \bar{x}_2) > 0\}$ if $(\bar{x}_1 - \bar{x}_2) > 0$ using the Excel code 1-NORM.DIST$((\bar{x}_1 - \bar{x}_2), 0, \sqrt{\frac{\sigma_1^2}{n_1} + \frac{\sigma_2^2}{n_2}}, 1)$. If either of these probabilities is $\leq \alpha/2$, the desired value for the probability that $(\bar{x}_1 - \bar{x}_2)$ falls below the margin of error or falls above the margin of error, reject the null hypothesis. Or else, do not reject the null hypothesis.

(b). $H_0: \mu_1 \geq \mu_2$ (or) $H_0: \mu_1 . \mu_2 \geq 0$

$H_1: \mu_1 < \mu_2$ (or) $H_1: \mu_1 - \mu_2 < 0$

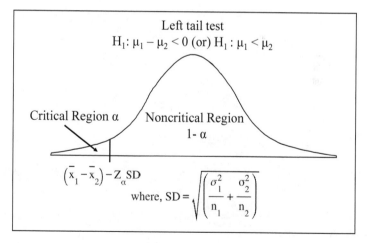

Left tail test
$H_1: \mu_1 - \mu_2 < 0$ (or) $H_1: \mu_1 < \mu_2$

Critical Region α Noncritical Region
$1 - \alpha$

$(\bar{x}_1 - \bar{x}_2) - Z_\alpha SD$
where, $SD = \sqrt{\left(\frac{\sigma_1^2}{n_1} + \frac{\sigma_2^2}{n_2} \right)}$

Find $\{P(\bar{x}_1 - \bar{x}_2) < 0\}$ using the Excel code NORM. DIST$((\bar{x}_1 - \bar{x}_2), 0, \sqrt{\frac{\sigma_1^2}{n_1} + \frac{\sigma_2^2}{n_2}})$. If $\{P(\bar{x}_1 - \bar{x}_2) < 0\}$ is less than α the null hypothesis is rejected. Or else, the null hypothesis is not rejected.

(c). $H_0: \mu_1 \leq \mu_2$ (or) $H_0: \mu_1 - \mu_2 \leq 0$

$H_1: \mu_1 > \mu_2$ (or) $H_1: \mu_1 - \mu_2 > 0$

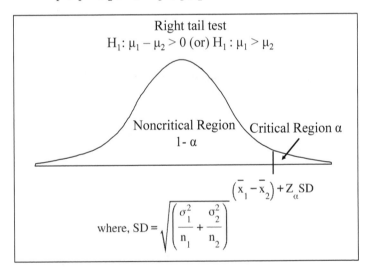

Find $1 - \{P(\bar{x}_1 - \bar{x}_2) > 0\}$ using the Excel code 1-NORM. DIST$((\bar{x}_1 - \bar{x}_2), 0, \sqrt{\frac{\sigma_1^2}{n_1} + \frac{\sigma_2^2}{n_2}}, 1)$. If $1 - \{P(\bar{x}_1 - \bar{x}_2) > 0\}$ is less than α the null hypothesis is rejected. Or else, the null hypothesis is not rejected.

Example

A reputed public school in Delhi has two mathematics teachers, Leena and Poonam. These two teachers have a very good track record over a decade with almost consistent average test scores with standard deviations of the scores five and nine respectively. In the current year, Leena has thirty-five students, Poonam has thirty-six students, and the average scores based on a standardized test for their students respectively are eighty-eight and ninety-five. Assuming the scores are normally distributed, do the sample results provide evidence that the two teachers are equally effective in their teaching?

The current year data may be considered as samples of the test scores of the students taught by the two teachers. The sample information given $n_1=35$, $n_2=36$, $\bar{x}_1=88$, $\bar{x}_2=95$, $\sigma_1=5$ and $\sigma_2=9$. The relevant hypotheses are:

H_0: The two teachers are equally effective in their teaching.

H_1: The two teachers are not equally effective in their teaching.

Alternatively:

H_0: $\mu_1 = \mu_2$ (or) H_0: $\mu_1-\mu_2 = 0$
H_1: $\mu_1 \neq \mu_2$ (or) H_1: $\mu_1-\mu_2 \neq 0$.

As $(\bar{x}_1 - \bar{x}_2) = 88-95 = -7$, find $\{P(\bar{x}_1-\bar{x}_2) < 0\}$ using the Excel code NORM.DIST$((\bar{x}_1-\bar{x}_2),0, \sqrt{\dfrac{\sigma_1^2}{n_1} + \dfrac{\sigma_2^2}{n_2}}, 1)$.

If $\{P(\bar{x}_1 - \bar{x}_2) < 0\}$ is less than $\alpha/2$ the null hypothesis is rejected. Or else, the null hypothesis is not rejected.

Here, $\sqrt{\dfrac{\sigma_1^2}{n_1} + \dfrac{\sigma_2^2}{n_2}} = \sqrt{\dfrac{5^2}{35} + \dfrac{9^2}{36}} = \sqrt{\dfrac{25}{35} + \dfrac{81}{36}} = 1.72171$.

Therefore, $\{P(\bar{x}_1 - \bar{x}_2) < 0\} = \text{NORM.DIST}(-7, 0,) = 0.000024 < 0.025$ (=$\alpha/2$). Hence, the null hypothesis is rejected and concluded in favour of the alternative hypothesis that the two teachers are not equally effective.

Two populations with unknown unequal variances

Assume that the two populations are of size N_1 and N_2 with means μ_1 and μ_2 with unknown unequal variances σ_1^2 and σ_2^2. Assume two samples are taken from these two populations with sizes n_1 and n_2 and their sample means, $\bar{x}_1$ and $\bar{x}_2$ are obtained. For large samples ($n_1 > 30$ and $n_2 > 30$) the difference of the sample means $(\bar{x}_1 - \bar{x}_2)$ will be normally distributed with a mean (μ_1, μ_2) and variance $\left(\dfrac{s_1^2}{n_1} + \dfrac{s_2^2}{n_2}\right)$ where $s_1^2 = \dfrac{1}{n_1 - 1}\sum_1^{n_1}\left(x_{1i} - \bar{x}_1\right)^2$ and $s_2^2 = \dfrac{1}{n_2 - 1}\sum_1^{n_2}\left(x_{2i} - \bar{x}_2\right)^2$ are unbiased estimators of σ_1^2 and σ_2^2 respectively.

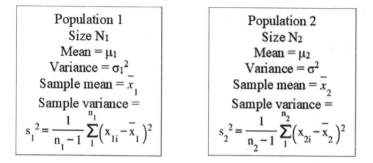

There are usually three possible sets of hypotheses.

(a). $H_0: \mu_1 = \mu_2$ (or) $H_0: \mu_1 . \mu_2 = 0$

$H_1: \mu_1 \neq \mu_2$ (or) $H_1: \mu_1 - \mu_2 \neq 0$

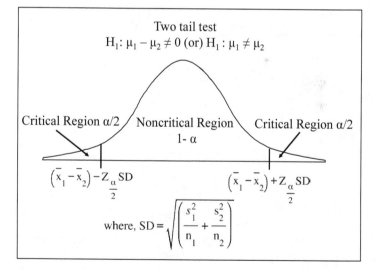

Find $\{P(\bar{x}_1 - \bar{x}_2) < 0\}$ if $(\bar{x}_1 - \bar{x}_2) < 0$ using the Excel code NORM.DIST$((\bar{x}_1 - \bar{x}_2), 0, \sqrt{\left(\frac{s_1^2}{n_1} + \frac{s_2^2}{n_2}\right)}, 1)$ or find $\{P(\bar{x}_1 - \bar{x}_2) > 0\}$ if $(\bar{x}_1 - \bar{x}_2) > 0$ using the Excel code 1-NORM.DIST$((\bar{x}_1 - \bar{x}_2), 0, \sqrt{\left(\frac{s_1^2}{n_1} + \frac{s_2^2}{n_2}\right)} 1)$. If either of these probabilities is $\leq \alpha/2$, the desired value for the probability that $(\bar{x}_1 - \bar{x}_2)$ falls below the margin of error or falls above the margin of error, reject the null hypothesis. Or else, do not reject the null hypothesis.

(b). $H_0: \mu_1 \geq \mu_2$ (or) $H_0: \mu_1 \_\mu_2 \geq 0$

$H_1: \mu_1 < \mu_2$ (or) $H_1: \mu_1 \text{-}\mu_2 < 0$

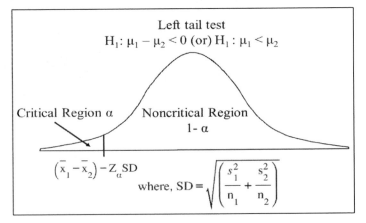

Left tail test
$H_1: \mu_1 - \mu_2 < 0$ (or) $H_1: \mu_1 < \mu_2$

Critical Region α　　Noncritical Region
$1 - \alpha$

$(\bar{x}_1 - \bar{x}_2) - Z_\alpha SD$

where, $SD = \sqrt{\left(\frac{s_1^2}{n_1} + \frac{s_2^2}{n_2}\right)}$

Find $\{P(\bar{x}_1 - \bar{x}_2) < 0\}$ using the Excel code NORM.DIST$((\bar{x}_1 - \bar{x}_2), 0, \sqrt{\left(\frac{s_1^2}{n_1} + \frac{s_2^2}{n_2}\right)}, 1)$. If $\{P(\bar{x}_1 - \bar{x}_2) < 0\}$ is less than α the null hypothesis is rejected. Or else, the null hypothesis is not rejected.

(c). H_0: $\mu_1 \leq \mu_2$ (or) H_0: $\mu_{1\text{-}}\mu_2 \leq 0$

H_1: $\mu_1 > \mu_2$ (or) H_1: $\mu_1\text{-}\mu_2 > 0$

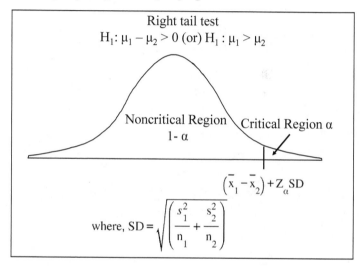

Find $1\text{-}\{P(\overline{x}_1\text{-}\overline{x}_2)>0\}$ using the Excel code 1-NORM. DIST$((\overline{x}_1\text{-}\overline{x}_2),0,\sqrt{\left(\frac{s_1^2}{n_1} + \frac{s_2^2}{n_2}\right)},1)$. If $1\text{-}\{P(\overline{x}_1\text{-}\overline{x}_2)>0\}$ is less than α the null hypothesis is rejected. Or else, the null hypothesis is not rejected.

Example

A power bank manufacturing company came out with a new type of power bank for mobile phones. The new type is expected to support mobile phones for a longer time than the old type manufactured by the same company. A simple random sample of fifty new type and old type power banks was tested. The old type of power bank continuously supported a mobile phone for an average of 360 minutes with a standard deviation of fifty-five minutes, and the new type of power bank continuously supported a mobile phone for an average of 420 minutes with a standard deviation of eighty minutes. The hypotheses to test the claim that the new type of power bank supports mobile phones for a longer period than the old type of power bank are:

H_0: The average support times of the old type of power bank and the new type of power bank are the same.

H_1: The average support time of the old type of power bank is less than the average support time of the new type of power bank

Alternatively:

H_0: $\mu_1 = \mu_2$ (or) H_0: $\mu_1 \cdot \mu_2 = 0$
H_1: $\mu_1 < \mu_2$ (or) H_1: $\mu_1 \cdot \mu_2 < 0$.

Given, $\bar{x}_1 = 360$, $\bar{x}_2 = 390$, $s_1 = 60$ and $s_2 = 90$, find $\{P(\bar{x}_1 \cdot \bar{x}_2) < 0\}$ using the Excel code NORM. DIST$((\bar{x}_1 \cdot \bar{x}_2), 0, \sqrt{\left(\frac{s_1^2}{n_1} + \frac{s_2^2}{n_2}\right)}, 1)$ = NORM.DIST(360-390,0,SQRT(60²/50+90²/50),1) = NORM.DIST(-30,0,SQRT(72+162),1) = 0.024930102 < 0.05 (α). Hence, reject the null hypothesis and conclude in favour of the alternative hypothesis. The claim of the manufacturer that the new type of power bank supports mobile phones for longer is valid based on the sample information.

Two populations with unknown equal variances small samples

Assume that the two populations are of size N_1 and N_2 with means μ_1 and μ_2 with unknown equal variances $\sigma_1^2 = \sigma_2^2 = \sigma^2$. Two small random samples ($n_1 < 30$ and $n_2 < 30$) are taken from the two populations. For small samples ($n_1 < 30$ and $n_2 < 30$) the difference of the sample means $(\bar{x}_1 - \bar{x}_2)$ will follow student t-distribution with a mean (μ_1, μ_2) and pooled variance

estimator $s_p^2 = \dfrac{(n_1 - 1)\sum_1^{n_1}(x_{1i} - \bar{x}_1)^2 + (n_2 - 1)\sum_1^{n_2}(x_{2i} - \bar{x}_2)^2}{n_1 + n_2 - 2}$, where

$s_1^2 = \dfrac{1}{n_1 - 1}\sum_1^{n_1}(x_{1i} - \bar{x}_1)^2$ and $s_2^2 = \dfrac{1}{n_2 - 1}\sum_1^{n_2}(x_{2i} - \bar{x}_2)^2$ are

unbiased estimators of σ_1^2 and σ_2^2 respectively.

Population 1
Size N_1
Mean = μ_1
Variance = σ^2
Sample mean = $\bar{x}_1$
Sample variance =
$s_1^2 = \dfrac{1}{n_1 - 1}\sum_1^{n_1}(x_{1i} - \bar{x}_1)^2$

Population 2
Size N_2
Mean = μ_2
Variance = σ^2
Sample mean = $\bar{x}_2$
Sample variance =
$s_2^2 = \dfrac{1}{n_2 - 1}\sum_1^{n_2}(x_{2i} - \bar{x}_2)^2$

There are usually three possible sets of hypotheses.

(a). $H_0: \mu_1 = \mu_2$ (or) $H_0: \mu_1 \mu_2 = 0$

$H_1: \mu_1 \neq \mu_2$ (or) $H_1: \mu_1 - \mu_2 \neq 0$

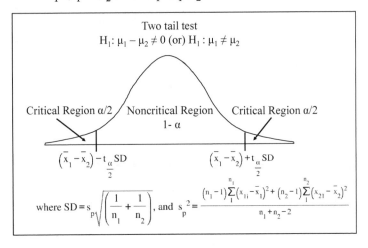

Find $\{P(\bar{x}_1 - \bar{x}_2) < 0\}$ if $(\bar{x}_1 - \bar{x}_2) < 0$ using the Excel code T.DIST(SQRT($(\bar{x}_1 - \bar{x}_2)/s_p\sqrt{\frac{1}{n_1} + \frac{1}{n_2}}$), $n_1 + n_2 - 2$, 1), or find $\{P(\bar{x}_1 - \bar{x}_2) > 0\}$ if $(\bar{x}_1 - \bar{x}_2) > 0$ using the Excel code 1- T.DIST(SQRT($(\bar{x}_1 - \bar{x}_2)/s_p\sqrt{\frac{1}{n_1} + \frac{1}{n_2}}$, $n_1 + n_2 - 2$, 1). If either of these probabilities is $\leq \alpha/2$, the desired value for the probability that $(\bar{x}_1 - \bar{x}_2)$ falls below the margin of error or falls above the margin of error, reject the null hypothesis. Or else, do not reject the null hypothesis.

(b). $H_0: \mu_1 \geq \mu_2$ (or) $H_0: \mu_1 \mu_2 \geq 0$

$H_1: \mu_1 < \mu_2$ (or) $H_1: \mu_1 - \mu_2 < 0$

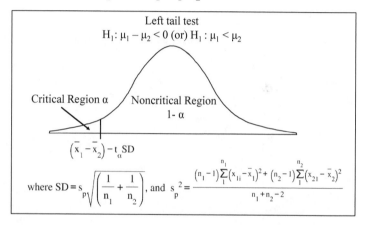

Find $\{P(\bar{x}_1 - \bar{x}_2) < 0\}$ using the Excel code T.DIST(SQRT$((\bar{x}_1 - \bar{x}_2)/s_p \sqrt{\frac{1}{n_1} + \frac{1}{n_2}})$, $n_1 + n_2 - 2, 1)$. If $\{P(\bar{x}_1 - \bar{x}_2) < 0\}$ is less than α, the null hypothesis is rejected. Or else, the null hypothesis is not rejected.

(c). $H_0: \mu_1 \leq \mu_2$ (or) $H_0: \mu_1 - \mu_2 \leq 0$

$H_1: \mu_1 > \mu_2$ (or) $H_1: \mu_1 - \mu_2 > 0$

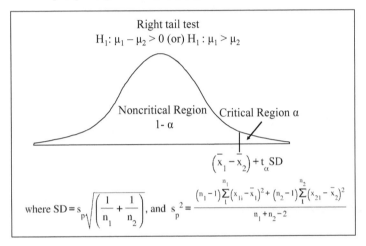

Find $1 - \{P(\bar{x}_1 - \bar{x}_2) > 0\}$ using the Excel code $1 - $ T.DIST(SQRT($(\bar{x}_1 - \bar{x}_2)/s_p\sqrt{\frac{1}{n_1} + \frac{1}{n_2}}$), $n_1 + n_2 - 2, 1$). If $1 - \{P(\bar{x}_1 - \bar{x}_2) > 0\}$ is less than α, the null hypothesis is rejected. Or else, the null hypothesis is not rejected.

Example

Two pharma companies manufacture insulin pills, one a generic pills manufacturer and the other a branded pills manufacturer. Pills manufactured by the branded company are currently in use and pills manufactured by the generic pills manufacturer are new. The pills manufactured by these two pharma companies are compared to determine their effect on blood sugar levels. As generic pills are cheaper, the same may be used for the treatment of type-2 diabetics if the average blood sugar levels of those taking the generic pills are the same as of those taking the branded pills. A clinical trial was conducted on eight patients, each with similar random blood sugar levels, and the results were, $\bar{x}_1$=92.255, $\bar{x}_2$=92.733, s_1=2.39, and s_2= 2.98.

The interest here is to see if the average blood sugar level is the same for those taking the generic pills and those taking the branded pills. The two hypotheses are:

H_0: The average blood sugar level is the same for those taking generic pills and those taking branded pills.

H_1: The average blood sugar level is not the same for those taking generic pills and those taking branded pills.

Alternatively stated:

H_0: $\mu_1 = \mu_2$ (or) H_0: $\mu_1 - \mu_2 = 0$
H_1: $\mu_1 \mu_2$ (or) H_0: $\mu_1 - \mu_2$ 0

Assuming equal variances in the two populations, the hypotheses can be tested using the t-distribution with the pooled estimate of the unknown variance. Since, $\bar{x}_1 - \bar{x}_2$ = 92.255 - 92.733 = - 0.478 < 0, find the

$\{P(\overline{x}_1 - \overline{x}_2) < 0\}$ using the Excel code T.DIST(SQRT(

$(\overline{x}_1 - \overline{x}_2)/s_p \sqrt{\dfrac{1}{n_1} + \dfrac{1}{n_2}})$, $n_1 + n_2 - 2, 1)$. As the alternative

hypothesis is two-sided, if $\{P(\overline{x}_1 - \overline{x}_2) < 0\}$ is less than or equal to $\alpha/2$, the null hypothesis is rejected. Here,

$$s_p^2 = \frac{(n_1 - 1)s_1^2 + (n_2 - 1)s_2^2}{n_1 + n_2 - 2} = \frac{7(2.39)^2 + 7(2.98)^2}{8 + 8 - 2} = 7.30.$$

Therefore, $s_p = 2.70$.

Thus, $P(\overline{x}_1 - \overline{x}_2) < 0 = $ T.DIST$((\overline{x}_1 - \overline{x}_2)/s_p \sqrt{\frac{1}{n_1} + \frac{1}{n_2}}$, $n_1 + n_2 - 2, 1)$

= T.DIST(-0.478/(2.70*SQRT(1/8 + 1/8)),14,1) = 0.36428 > 0.025.

Hence, the null hypothesis is not rejected, and it is concluded that the average blood sugar level is the same for those taking the generic pills and those taking the branded pills. If the generic pills are cheaper, the same may be adopted.

Two population proportions with unequal variances

Suppose that there are two populations with unknown binomial parameters of interest, say p_1 and p_2 with unequal variances $\frac{p_1(1-p_1)}{n_1} = \frac{p_2(1-p_2)}{n_2}$. Two independent random samples of sizes n_1 and n_2 are taken from two populations, and let x_1 and x_2 represent the number of observations that belong to the class of interest in the two samples. The unbiased estimates of the unknown binomial parameters are $\hat{p}_1 = \bar{p}_1 = \dfrac{x_1}{n_1}$ and $\hat{p}_2 = \bar{p}_2 = \dfrac{x_2}{n_2}$. The variances of the sample proportions are $V(\bar{p}_1) = \dfrac{\bar{p}_1(1-\bar{p}_1)}{n_1}$ and $V(\bar{p}_2) = \dfrac{\bar{p}_2(1-\bar{p}_2)}{n_2}$.

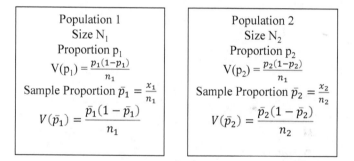

There are usually three possible sets of hypotheses.

(a). $H_0: p_1 = p_2$ (or) $H_0: p_1\text{-}p_2 = 0$

$H_1: p_1 < p_2$ (or) $H_1: p_1\text{-}p_2 < 0$

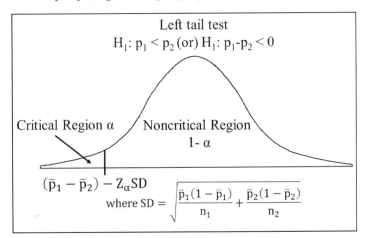

Find $\{P(\bar{p}_1 - \bar{p}_2) < 0\}$ using the Excel code $NORM.DIST((\bar{p}_1 - \bar{p}_2), 0, \sqrt{\frac{\bar{p}_1(1-\bar{p}_1)}{n_1} + \frac{\bar{p}_2(1-\bar{p}_2)}{n_2}}, 1)$. If $\{P(\bar{p}_1 - \bar{p}_2) < 0\} \leq \alpha$, the desired value for the probability that falls below the margin of error, reject the null hypothesis. Or else, do not reject the null hypothesis.

(b). H$_0$: p$_1 \geq$ p$_2$ (or) H$_0$: p$_1$_p$_2 \geq$ 0

H$_1$: p$_1 >$ p$_2$ (or) H$_1$: p$_1$-p$_2 >$ 0

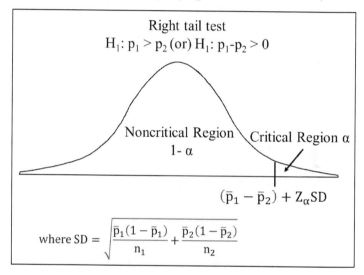

Find $\{P(\bar{p}_1 - \bar{p}_2) > 0\}$ using the Excel code 1-NORM.DIST$((\bar{p}_1 - \bar{p}_2), 0, \sqrt{\frac{\bar{p}_1(1-\bar{p}_1)}{n_1} + \frac{\bar{p}_2(1-\bar{p}_2)}{n_2}}, 1)$. Reject the null hypothesis if $\{P(\bar{p}_1 - \bar{p}_2) > 0\} \leq \alpha$, the desired value for the probability that $(\bar{p}_1 - \bar{p}_2)$ falls above the margin of error. Else, do not reject the null hypothesis.

(c). $H_0\colon p_1 \le p_2$ (or) $H_0\colon p_1\text{-}p_2 \le 0$

$H_1\colon p_1 \ne p_2$ (or) $H_1\colon p_1\text{-}p_2 \ne 0$

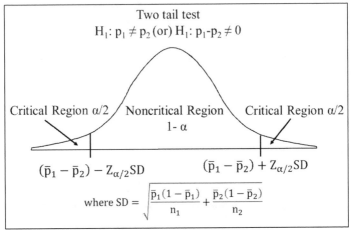

Find $\{P(\bar{p}_1 - \bar{p}_2) < 0\}$ if $(\bar{p}_1 - \bar{p}_2) < 0$ using the Excel code $\text{NORM.DIST}((\bar{p}_1 - \bar{p}_2), 0,$ $\sqrt{\frac{\bar{p}_1(1-\bar{p}_1)}{n_1} + \frac{\bar{p}_2(1-\bar{p}_2)}{n_2}}, 1)$ or find $\{P(\bar{p}_1 - \bar{p}_2) > 0\}$ if $(\bar{p}_1 - \bar{p}_2) > 0$ using the Excel code $1\text{-} \text{NORM.DIST}($ $(\bar{p}_1 - \bar{p}_2), 0, \sqrt{\frac{\bar{p}_1(1-\bar{p}_1)}{n_1} + \frac{\bar{p}_2(1-\bar{p}_2)}{n_2}}, 1)$. If either of these probabilities is $\le \alpha/2$, the desired value for the probability that $(\bar{p}_1 - \bar{p}_2)$ falls below the margin of error or falls above the margin of error, reject the null hypothesis. Or else, do not reject the null hypothesis.

Example

A leading piston rings manufacturing company has two production plants A and B in two locations in the country. The two plants produce identical products and follow strict quality control norms. A sample of 200 units from plant A showed 10 per cent were non-conforming, and a sample of 300 units from plant B showed 15 per cent were non-conforming. Based on these sample results, can it be concluded that production plant A is doing a better job than production plant B?

The two production plants may be assumed to have unequal variances for the proportion of non-conforming products. Given the sample results, $\bar{p}_1 = 0.10$ and $\bar{p}_2 = 0.15$, the hypotheses tested are:

H_0: The performance of production plants A and B are the same.

H_1: The performance of production plant A is better than that of production plant B.

Alternatively:

H_0: $p_1 = p_2$ (or) H_0: $p_1 \cdot p_2 = 0$
H_1: $p_1 < p_2$ (or) H_1: $p_1 - p_2 < 0$

Find $\{P(\bar{p}_1 - \bar{p}_2) < 0\}$ using the Excel code $NORM.DIST((\bar{p}_1 - \bar{p}_2), 0, \sqrt{\frac{\bar{p}_1(1-\bar{p}_1)}{n_1} + \frac{\bar{p}_2(1-\bar{p}_2)}{n_2}}$, 1). If $\{P(\bar{p}_1 - \bar{p}_2) < 0\} \leq \alpha$, the desired value for the probability that $(\bar{p}_1 - \bar{p}_2)$ falls below the margin of error, reject the null hypothesis. Or else, do not reject the null hypothesis. Given, $\bar{p}_1 = 0.10$ and $\bar{p}_2 = 0.15$, $\bar{p}_1 - \bar{p}_2 = -0.05$, $\frac{\bar{p}_1(1-\bar{p}_1)}{n_1} = \frac{0.10*0.90}{200} = 0.00045$, $\frac{\bar{p}_2(1-\bar{p}_2)}{n_2} = \frac{0.15*0.85}{300} = 0.000425$ and $\sqrt{\frac{\bar{p}_1(1-\bar{p}_1)}{n_1} + \frac{\bar{p}_2(1-\bar{p}_2)}{n_2}} = \sqrt{0.00045 + 0.000425} = 0.02958$.

Hence, $\{P(\bar{p}_1 - \bar{p}_2) < 0\} = NORM.DIST((\bar{p}_1 - \bar{p}_2),0,\sqrt{\frac{\bar{p}_1(1-\bar{p}_1)}{n_1} + \frac{\bar{p}_2(1-\bar{p}_2)}{n_2}},1) = $ NORM.DIST(-0.05,0,0.02958,1) $= 0.045482 < 0.05$ (α). Hence the null hypothesis is rejected and concluded in favour of the alternative hypothesis that plant A is doing a better job.

Two population proportions with equal variances

Suppose that there are two populations with unknown binomial parameters of interest, say p_1 and p_2 with equal variances $\frac{p_1(1-p_1)}{n_1} = \frac{p_2(1-p_2)}{n_2} = \frac{p(1-p)}{n}$. Two independent random samples of sizes n_1 and n_2 are taken from two populations, and let x_1 and x_2 represent the number of observations that belong to the class of interest in the two samples. The unbiased estimates of the unknown binomial parameters are $\hat{p}_1 = \bar{p}_1 = \frac{x_1}{n_1}$, $\hat{p}_2 = \bar{p}_2 = \frac{x_2}{n_2}$, and

$\hat{p} = \bar{p} = \dfrac{x_1 + x_2}{n_1 + n_2}$. The variance of the combined sample proportion is $V(\bar{p}) = \bar{p}(1-\bar{p})\left(\dfrac{1}{n_1} + \dfrac{1}{n_2}\right)$.

Population 1
Size N_1
Proportion p_1
Sample Proportion $\bar{p}_1 = \frac{x_1}{n_1}$

Population 2
Size N_2
Proportion p_2
Sample Proportion $\bar{p}_2 = \frac{x_2}{n_2}$

There are usually three possible sets of hypotheses.

(a). H_0: $p_1 \geq p_2$ (or) H_0: $p_1\_p_2 \geq 0$

H_1: $p_1 < p_2$ (or) H_1: p_1-$p_2 < 0$

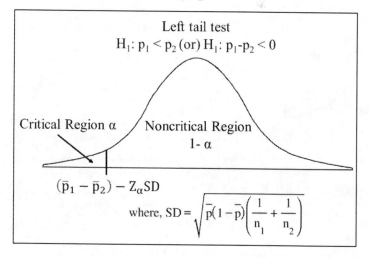

Left tail test
H_1: $p_1 < p_2$ (or) H_1: p_1-$p_2 < 0$

Critical Region α Noncritical Region
$1 - \alpha$

$(\bar{p}_1 - \bar{p}_2) - Z_\alpha SD$

where, $SD = \sqrt{\bar{p}(1-\bar{p})\left(\dfrac{1}{n_1} + \dfrac{1}{n_2}\right)}$

Find $\{P(\bar{p}_1 - \bar{p}_2) < 0\}$ using the Excel code

$$\text{NORM.DIST}\left((\bar{p}_1 - \bar{p}_2), 0, \sqrt{\bar{p}(1-\bar{p})\left(\frac{1}{n_1} + \frac{1}{n_2}\right)}\, 1\right).$$

If $\{P(\bar{p}_1 - \bar{p}_2) < 0\} \leq \alpha$, the desired value for the probability that $(\bar{p}_1 - \bar{p}_2)$ falls below the margin of error, reject the null hypothesis. Or else, do not reject the null hypothesis.

(b). $H_0: p_1 \leq p_2$ (or) $H_0: p_1\text{-}p_2 \leq 0$

$H_1: p_1 > p_2$ (or) $H_1: p_1\text{-}p_2 > 0$

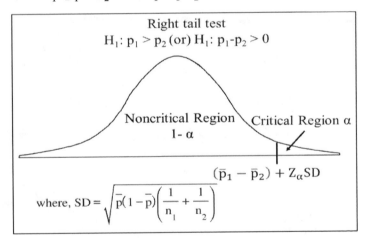

Find $\{P(\bar{p}_1 - \bar{p}_2) > 0\}$ using the Excel code

$$1\text{-}\text{NORM.DIST}\left((\bar{p}_1 - \bar{p}_2), 0, \sqrt{\bar{p}(1-\bar{p})\left(\frac{1}{n_1} + \frac{1}{n_2}\right)}\right.$$

1). If $\{P(\bar{p}_1 - \bar{p}_2)>0\} \leq \alpha$, the desired value for the probability that $(\bar{p}_1 - \bar{p}_2)$ falls above the margin of error, reject the null hypothesis. Or else, do not reject the null hypothesis.

(c). H_0: $p_1 = p_2$ (or) H_0: $p_1.p_2 = 0$

H_1: $p_1 \neq p_2$ (or) H_1: $p_1\text{-}p_2 \neq 0$

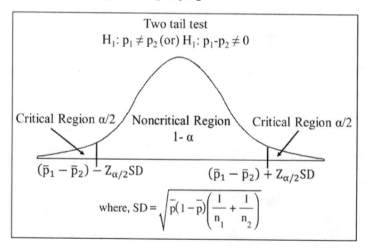

Find $\{P(\bar{p}_1 - \bar{p}_2) < 0 \}$ if $(\bar{p}_1 - \bar{p}_2) < 0$ using the Excel code NORM.DIST$((\bar{p}_1 - \bar{p}_2),0,$ $\sqrt{\bar{p}(1-\bar{p})\left(\dfrac{1}{n_1} + \dfrac{1}{n_2}\right)},1)$ or find $\{P(\bar{p}_1 - \bar{p}_2)>0\}$ if $(\bar{p}_1 - \bar{p}_2)>0$ using the Excel code 1- NORM.DIST $((\bar{p}_1 - \bar{p}_2),0,$ $\sqrt{\bar{p}(1-\bar{p})\left(\dfrac{1}{n_1} + \dfrac{1}{n_2}\right)},1)$. If either of these probabilities is $\leq \alpha/2$, the desired value for the probability that $(\bar{p}_1 - \bar{p}_2)$ falls below the margin of error or falls above the margin of error, reject the null hypothesis. Or else, do not reject the null hypothesis.

Example

Suppose a biotech company develops a new vaccine to prevent the coronavirus. The company states that the vaccine is equally effective for men and women. To test this claim, simple random samples of 100 women and 200 men from a population of 1,00,000 volunteers were selected and administered the vaccine. At the end of the study, 20 per cent of the women caught the virus and 35 per cent of the men caught the virus. Do these results support the claim of the company that the vaccine is equally effective for men and women?

The proportion of interest here is the proportion of people affected by the coronavirus. As the samples are taken from the same population of volunteers and the company's claim is that the vaccine is equally effective for both men and women, the equal variance of the proportions of men and women affected by coronavirus can be assumed. Let p_1 be the proportion of women affected by the coronavirus and p_2 be the proportion of men affected by the coronavirus. Given the sample information,

$$\hat{p}_1 = \bar{p}_1 = 0.20, \quad \hat{p}_2 = \bar{p}_2 = 0.35, \quad \text{and} \quad \hat{p} = \bar{p} = \frac{20 + 70}{300} = 0.30.$$

The variance of the combined sample proportion is $V(\bar{p}) = 0.3(1-0.7)\left(\dfrac{1}{100} + \dfrac{1}{200}\right) = 0.00315$ and the SD=$\sqrt{(0.00315)}$ = 0.056125. The hypotheses are:

H_0: The vaccine is equally effective for men and women.

H_1: The vaccine is not equally effective for men and women.

Alternatively:

H_0: $p_1 = p_2$ (or) H_0: $p_1 . p_2 = 0$
H_1: $p_1 \neq p_2$ (or) H_1: $p_1 - p_2 \neq 0$

As $(\bar{p}_1 - \bar{p}_2)$ = -0.15<0, find the $\{P(\bar{p}_1 - \bar{p}_2) < 0\}$ using the Excel code NORM.DIST(-0.15,0,0.056125,1) = 0.003763. As $\{P(\bar{p}_1 - \bar{p}_2) < 0\}$ < 0.025 ($\alpha/2$) reject the null hypothesis and conclude that the vaccine is not equally effective.

The one-tailed hypothesis is appropriate here.

H_0: The vaccine is equally effective for men and women.

H_1: The vaccine is more effective for women than men.

Alternatively:

H_0: $p_1 = p_2$ (or) H_0: $p_1 . p_2 = 0$
H_1: $p_1 < p_2$ (or) H_1: $p_1 - p_2 < 0$

As the $P(\bar{p}_1 - \bar{p}_2) < 0\} = 0.003763 < 0.05$ (α) the null hypothesis is rejected and concluded in favour of the alternative hypothesis. That is, the vaccine is more effective for women than men.

Two populations paired t-test

In certain medical, scientific and biotech laboratory experiments, training programmes organized by companies, vaccination programmes, and experiments involving before and after-effects like weight loss or weight gain programmes, etc., it is of interest to see if the average of differences in the measurements before and after the training programme is zero. In this kind of situation, each unit in the sample will have a pair of measurements, one *before* and another *after*. The observations are dependent as they are measured from the same units, maybe at two different time points. Suppose a sample of n units is considered for a study of this kind. When there are two samples in which observations from one sample can be paired with observations from the other sample, a paired t-test is used to compare two population means. A couple of examples are before-and-after observations on the same subjects (e.g., diagnostic test results before and after a specific training) and a comparison of two distinct methods of measurement or two different treatments applied to the same subjects (e.g., blood pressure measurements using a stethoscope and a dynamap).

Assume that x_{11}, x_{12}, x_{13}, . . ., x_{1n} and x_{21}, x_{22}, x_{23}, . . ., x_{2n} are the two sets of observations. Then to check if there is any differences in the two methods considered, the differences of these observations, $(x_{11}\text{-}x_{21}=z_1)$, $(x_{12}\text{-}x_{22}=z_2)$, $(x_{13}\text{-}x_{23}=z_3)$, . . . , $(x_{1n}\text{-}x_{2n}=z_n)$ are used. The sample mean $\bar{z} = \dfrac{\sum z}{n}$ and the standard deviation of z, $s_z = \sqrt{\dfrac{1}{n-1}\sum(z_i - \bar{z})^2}$ are obtained. As most experiments of this kind are usually conducted on a small sample, a t-test is used. This t-test is named paired t-test because a pair of observations for each unit in the sample is used.

Let μ_D be the mean of such differences in the population (always the first minus the second $\mu_1\text{-}\mu_2$). The three sets of the hypotheses are given below.

(a). $H_0 : \mu_D \geq 0$; $H_1 : \mu_D < 0$

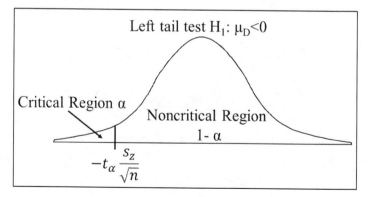

To test this hypothesis, find the $P(\bar{z} < 0)$ using the Excel code T.DIST($\bar{z}$/SD, n-1,1) where SD = $s_z/\sqrt{n}$. If this probability is $\leq \alpha$, the desired value for the probability that $\bar{x}$ exceeds the margin of error, reject the null hypothesis. Or else, do not reject the null hypothesis.

Example

Ten type-2 diabetic patients were treated with a combination of medicine, diet and exercise. Fasting blood sugar level (FBS) in mg/dL of these ten patients before and after six months into the treatment programme was compiled to study the effectiveness of the treatment. Using the information given below, test if the treatment programme was effective in lowering the FBS.

FBS values after 6 months - mg/dL	101	124	117	112	99	126	118	114	120	135
Initial FBS values - mg/dL	155	176	135	145	134	178	167	154	160	179
z	-54	-52	-18	-33	-35	-52	-49	-40	-40	-44

To test if the treatment programme was effective in lowering the FBS, the following hypotheses are tested:

H_0: The treatment programme was not effective in lowering the FBS.

H_1: The treatment programme was effective in lowering the FBS.

Alternatively, H_0: $\mu_D \geq 0$ against the alternative H_1: $\mu_D < 0$.

From the given data, $\bar{z}$ = -41.7, s_z = 11.1060544, n=10, and S.D = 3.512042774. Find $P(\bar{z} < 0)$ using the Excel code DIST($\bar{z}$/SD,n-1,1) where SD = $s_z/\sqrt{n}$. That is, $P(\bar{z} < 0)$ = T.DIST(-41.7/3.512042774,9,1) = 0.00000042 < 0.05 (α). Hence, the null hypothesis is rejected. It may be concluded that the treatment programme was effective in lowering the FBS.

(b). H_0: $\mu_D \leq 0$; H_1: $\mu_D > 0$

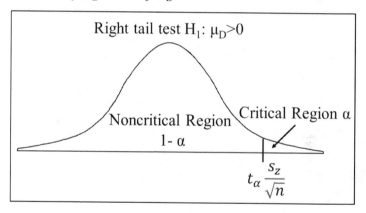

To test this hypothesis, find the $P(\bar{z} > 0)$ using the Excel code 1-T.DIST($\bar{z}$/SD, n-1,1) where SD = $s_z/\sqrt{n}$. If this probability is $\leq \alpha$, the desired value for the probability that x̄ falls below the margin of error, reject the null hypothesis. Or else, do not reject the null hypothesis.

Example

Consider a batch of twelve adults undergoing a rigorous weight-loss treatment programme for six months. The details regarding their weights in kilograms before and after the treatment programme are taken and tested to determine the effectiveness of the programme.

Weight before	102	98	78	89	66	72	110	92	69	77	79	88
Weight after	98	96	79	81	71	68	106	88	72	73	76	86

To see if the treatment programme was effective, the following hypotheses are tested:

H_0: The weight loss programme was not effective. There is no difference in the average weights of the adults before and after the programme.

H_1: The weight loss treatment programme was effective. The average weight of the adults after the programme is less than the average weight of the adults before the programme.

Alternatively, H_0: $\mu_D \leq 0$ against the alternative H_1: $\mu_D > 0$.

The hypotheses are tested using the probability that $P(\bar{z} > 0)$ using the Excel code 1-T.DIST($\bar{z}$/SD, n-1,1) where SD $= s_z / \sqrt{n}$. From the given data on the weights before and after, $\bar{z} = 2.17$, $s_z = 3.563280749$, n=12, and S.D$=1.028631, P(\bar{z} > 0) = 1$-T.DIST($2.17/1.028631, 11, 1$) $= 0.029308732$. Since $P(\bar{z} > 0) = 0.029308732 < 0.05$ (α) reject the null hypothesis and conclude in favour of the alternative hypothesis. The weight loss treatment programme was effective.

(c). $H_0: \mu_D = 0$; $H_1: \mu_D \neq 0$

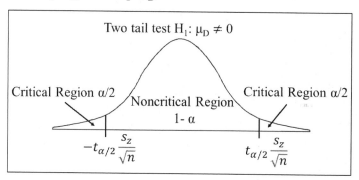

To test this hypothesis, find either the $P(\bar{z}<0)$ using the Excel code T.DIST($\bar{z}$/SD, n-1,1) or $P(\bar{z}>0)$ using the Excel code 1-T.DIST($\bar{z}$/SD, n-1,1) where SD = $s_z/\sqrt{n}$. If either of these probabilities is $\leq \alpha/2$, the desired value for the probability that $\bar{x}$ falls below the margin of error or falls above the margin of error, reject the null hypothesis. Or else, do not reject the null hypothesis.

Example

A general physician conducted an experiment involving ten sets of identical twins who were born fifteen years ago. He measured their weights in kilograms according to which twin was born first and second. The details are given in the table. The physician wants to check if there is a statistically significant difference between weights the first born and second born of the twins.

Twin set	1	2	3	4	5	6	7	8	9	10
1st born	42	39	29	36	49	37	39	38	51	44
2nd born	44	43	28	39	51	39	42	42	44	44

Can the physician infer that there is a significant difference in weight between the twins?

To see if the twins differ in their weights, the following hypotheses are tested.

H_0: There is no difference in weight between the twins.

H_1: There is a difference in weight between the twins.

Alternatively, H_0: $\mu_D = 0$ against the alternative H_1: $\mu_D \neq 0$.

From the given data, $\bar{z}=-1.2$, $s_z=3.293090409$, n=10, and S.D=1.041366623. Since $\bar{z}$ is negative, find $P(\bar{z} < 0)$ using the Excel code T.DIST($\bar{z}$/SD, n-1,1) where SD = $s_z/\sqrt{n}$. That is, $P(\bar{z} < 0)$ = T.DIST(-1.2/1.041366623,9,1) = 0.139436 > 0.025 ($\alpha/2$). Hence the null hypothesis is not rejected. Therefore, the physician can infer that there is no difference in weight between the twins.

All three possible cases of hypotheses are discussed throughout the testing of hypotheses with appropriate examples. In practice, only one alternative hypothesis is tested. The selection of the right alternative hypothesis is an art that comes with experience. The hypothesis that needs to be proved or established is the alternative hypothesis. It is reiterated here that the alternative hypothesis is decided first. The null hypothesis is decided automatically as the complement of the alternative hypothesis. The test procedure depends on the alternative hypothesis.

5

Regression—Building Relationships

Model building

Consider the construction of a spring balance. The spring balance shows the weight of an object through the length of a spring attached to the balance pulled by the weight of an object. The figure below illustrates this.

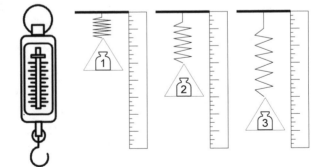

The weight and the length are two ways related. That is, weight depends on the length and the length depends on the weight. As the length and weight are directly related, the relationship between them can be considered linear, represented by the equation:

$$l = a + bw$$

where l is the length of the spring and w is the weight of an object being measured, a is the intercept and b is the regression coefficient that gives the rate of change of length relative to the weight. This means that one unit of change in weight will produce b units of change in length.

The regression between the length of the spring and the weight can be used in modelling as well as in calibrating the instrument. Determine the weight of a sample (for instance, ten mangoes) using the instrument. To use it as a reliable instrument, the same needs to be calibrated. That is, find a relationship between the measured parameter (length) and the unknown parameter (weight). Here is how this can be done:

- Perform a series of experiments with known weights, and measure the length of the spring for each experiment.
- Collect all observations into a data table, and analyse data using simple linear regression. That is, find the straight line that comes as close as possible

to all observed points, and then approximate observed values with fitted values along that line. To do this mathematically, compute the values of the two variables, slope and intercept, that define the regression line. The mathematical relationship $w = a + b*l$ is called a model. Once this model is created the same can be used for predictions.

• When the values of 'a' and 'b' are calculated, the instrument is calibrated. The instrument can be used to determine the weight of the test sample. All that needs to be done is to measure the new spring length, then feed its value into the model equation, which will yield the approximate weight of the sample.

Linear regression model

The linear regression model is the simple model that depicts the relationship between two variables X and Y. The equation that describes how Y is related to X and an error term (residual represented by ε) is called the regression model. The simple linear regression model is:

$$Y = \beta_0 + \beta_1 X + \varepsilon$$

In the model, the variable X is known as the independent variable or explanatory variable, and Y is the dependent variable or the explained variable. The constants β_0 and β_1 are called parameters of the model, ε is a random variable called the error term, which is the residual $(Y-\widehat{Y})$.

The estimated simple linear regression equation is, where b_0 is the y intercept of the line, b_1 is the slope of the line, and is the estimated value of y for a given x value. The values of b_0 and b_1 are obtained using the principle of least squares. That is, by minimizing $\sum(y_i-\widehat{Y})^2$. For the simple linear regression, $b_1 = \dfrac{\sum_1^n \left(x_i - \overline{x}\right)\left(y_i - \overline{y}\right)}{\sum_1^n \left(x_i - \overline{x}\right)^2}$, and

$b_0 = \overline{y} - b_1 \overline{x}$.

Example

Continuing with the spring balance example, let a sample of nine observations on the weight of an object and the respective length of the spring be as given in the table below.

| Weight | 1 | 1.5 | 2 | 2.5 | 3 | 3.5 | 4 | 4.5 | 6 |
| Length | 15 | 17 | 18.2 | 19.5 | 21 | 23 | 25 | 26.5 | 27 |

Assuming the length of the spring depends on the weight, the regression equation of the length as a function of the weight is obtained based on the sample values as, l=13.152+2.637w. The regression coefficient of length on weight is 2.637. That is, for every unit change in weight there is a 2.637 unit change in length expected. The correlation coefficient between the length of the spring and the mass is 0.969. The coefficient of determination is 0.939. This shows that about 94 per cent of the variations in the length are explained by the variations in mass. Standard analytical packages like Excel produce the coefficients as well as a graphical output for a visual understanding.

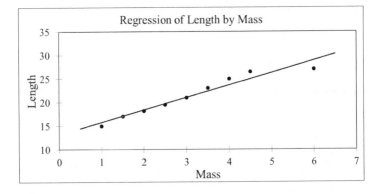

In real-life situations, regression is used in predictions for business projection. The reliability of the regression is studied by the residuals, the difference between the actual values and the predicted values using the regression equation. Residuals are the distance between the original position of the objects and their position on the projection map. If a scatter plot of residuals shows a close concentration of the residuals around the zero axis, the regression is a good predictor. The residual plot for the spring balance example above is given below.

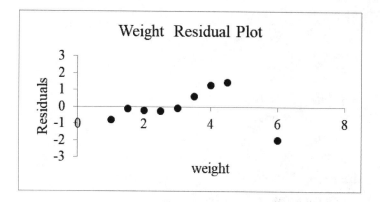

The residual plots are scattered well around the zero axis and do not show any pattern or trend. Hence the regression equation can be used to predict the length of the spring for any given weight of an object. The length in a spring balance reads the value of the weight of an object.

Testing of hypothesis for the regression coefficient

The significance of the regression is usually understood by testing for the regression coefficient. The null hypothesis is the regression coefficient is zero against the alternative the regression coefficient is not zero. That is,

$$H_0: \beta = 0 \text{ against } H_1 = \beta \neq 0.$$

Like any other testing of hypotheses, there are three alternatives possible. They are:

(a). H_0: $\beta = 0$ against $H_1 = \beta \neq 0$

(b). H_0: $\beta = 0$ against $H_1 = \beta > 0$

(c). H_0: $\beta = 0$ against $H_1 = \beta < 0$

The cases (b) and (c) indicate whether the relationship is positive or negative. In practical situations, a positive relationship is understood if the regression coefficient is positive, and a negative relationship is understood if the regression coefficient is negative. Hence, only the alternative hypothesis (a) is tested.

The hypothesis is tested using the t-statistic, $t = \dfrac{b}{s_b}$, where 'b' is the regression coefficient and s_b is the standard error of the regression coefficient. Here, $s_b = 0.253021088$. Reject the null hypothesis if the computed value of 't' is greater than or equal to $t\alpha_{/2}$ where $t\alpha_{/2}$ can be found using the Excel code T.INV($\alpha/2$, n-1) where n is the number of observations. Here the computed value of t= 2.636871508/ 0.253021088 = 10.4215484, and T.INV(0.975, 8) = 2.306. The null hypothesis is rejected, and it is concluded that the regression coefficient is not zero, and hence the relationship between weight and length is significant.

Alternatively, the entire linear regression analysis can be done using Excel. The steps are,

MENU → DATA → DATA ANALYSIS → REGRESSION and input the data as required in the pop-up window. Detailed results of the regression are displayed. The following is an excerpt from the detailed analysis report.

Value of the coefficient of determination R^2 = 0.939450908014151. This means that about 94 per cent of the variations in the length are explained by weight. Also available are the values of the regression coefficients, and the associated 't' and 'p' values as shown in the table below.

	Coefficients	Standard error	t-Statistic	p-value
Intercept	13.15195531	0.872423497	15.0751961	0.00000136
Weight	2.636871508	0.253021088	10.4215484	0.00001629

The p-values are the probabilities of the computed values of 't' exceeding the desired value of $t_{\alpha/2}$.

Multiple linear regression

Multiple linear regression (MLR) simultaneously considers the influence of multiple explanatory variables, say $X_1, X_2, \ldots, X_k$ on a response variable, Y. Let n observations be taken on each of the X variables and Y variable. The intent is to look at the independent effect of each variable.

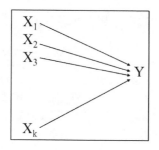

MLR aims at finding a linear relationship between Y and the Xs. Mathematically, this translates as:

$$Y = \beta_0 + \beta_1 X_1 + \ldots + \beta_k X_k + e$$

Using matrix notation, the same is written as:

$$Y = Xb + e$$

Here, 'e' is the part of Y that cannot be modelled as a function of the Xs (e is termed the residual).

Geometrically, this translates as trying to fit a line (when there is a single X variable) or a plane (when there are 2) or a hyperplane as close as possible to the observations (points that have the Xs as first coordinates and the Y value as of last coordinate). The projections on that plane are called fitted values ($y = b_0 + b_1 x_1 + \ldots + b_k x_k$), and each observation has a residual, which is $e = y - \hat{y}$. The criterion of closeness between observed and fitted values is called the least squares criterion, the plane should lie where it minimizes the sum of squares of all residuals.

Based on the least squares' criterion, the estimates of β coefficients are obtained as:

$$\hat{\beta} = \hat{\beta} = (X'X)^{-1}X'Y$$

Estimation of these coefficients can be done using any software or openly available tools like R, MATLAB,

Julia, or Python. Similar inferences as that of linear regression can be drawn. This method works well if the X variables are independent of each other. If some of the X variables are related (case of collinearity), there is a chance that some of the coefficients may not be estimated with sufficient precision. MLR is also sensitive to noise, i.e., random variation, in the variables. Furthermore, MLR cannot be applied when the number of X variables is more than the number of observations.

Principal component regression

Principal component regression (PCR) is simply a combination of principal components analysis (PCA) and MLR. Its primary use is to solve the problem of collinearity. Instead of using the X variables directly in the regression, first, the X matrix is modelled with PCA, and the PCs (which are independent of, or orthogonal to, each other) are used as new predictors in an MLR. It also solves the problem of more variables than observations. But there is no guarantee that all the information extracted from the X matrix by the PC model is relevant to Y.

Partial least squares or projected latent structures (PLS) regression

PLS regression looks a bit like 2 PCAs performed separately on the X and Y matrices, with a further constraint that each component extracted from the Y matrix should be as 'correlated' as possible to the corresponding component extracted from the X matrix. PLS is also a projection method, but it focuses on extracting from the X matrix only the share of information that is relevant to Y. The objective is to maximize the covariance between X and Y. Thus, it generally produces more economic models, which are easier to interpret.

Logistic regression

Regression is building a relationship between two or more quantitative variables. It is not easy to deal with regression among qualitative or categorical variables. Sometimes, the use of dummy variables is recommended. This is true in the case of male or female type variables and sensory variables. Out of several possible approaches, logistic regression is one of the most widely used methods in the analytics world.

If the dependent variable (target) is categorical, logistic regression is used. It is a method for calculating the likelihood of a discrete outcome given a set of input variables. This sort of statistical analysis is frequently applied in predictive analytics and modelling, as well as machine learning applications. The dependent variable is either finite or categorical such as either A or B (binary) or a range of finite possibilities A, B, C or D (categorical). Logistic regression is a method of calculating the probability of a given event occurring. Logistic regression models the relationship between one dependent binary variable and one or more nominal, ordinal, interval or ratio-level independent variables. The most common logistic regression models a binary outcome such as whether an email is spam (1) or (0) not spam, whether a tumour is malignant (1) or not (0), true (1) or false (0), yes (1) or no (0), and so on. A simple example would be to see how likely it is for someone to eat an ice cream on a hot summer day given the temperature is thirty-six degrees centigrade. This is a simple yes/no prediction.

One sees the extensive application of the binary classification in daily life. Some applications are obvious while others are not so obvious.

1. Today, all financial institutions battle a severe problem—trying to determine if a credit card transaction was made by the owner, or if a fraudster had done the same with compromised customer information. One has heard of instances where someone paid Rs 20,000 for a pizza or someone lost Rs 50,000 on a PayTm transfer and so on. Sometimes banks do call customers to verify if a transaction of a high value was initiated by the owner of the card before authorizing the credit/ debit card for the transaction. The objective here is simple. Given a customer's information (data/ facts), figuring out if the transaction is genuine or

fraudulent. The idea of a safe zone is still valid, but the interest is more on understanding if the behaviour of the individual of interest has deviated from the safe zone.

2. Another application of a binary classification system is to figure out the ability of a customer to pay the monthly instalments if credit was offered based on their information and transactional background. A bank desires to increase its consumer base as much as possible, but the business demands customers who are capable of paying back.

3. With advances in technology, many start-ups are promising superfast delivery of food. One such binary classification problem is to understand which customer is likely to purchase a particular food item so that businesses are better prepared to serve and at the same time keep operating costs low. For example, Swiggy or Zomato can save lakhs of rupees just by knowing whether a customer is going to order in the next hour and what food item they are likely to order. This allows them to pre-order items in bulk at a discounted price and be able to service the customer in a very short period.

4. People spend a lot of time on the internet searching for information or purchasing products, for example, searching for a good restaurant that offers a Friday night dinner at special prices, or looking up which movies are playing, or buying a pair of sneakers on Amazon. It may be seen that

often customers are approached to rate, review or provide feedback, and such reviews and feedback are also used to decide on the purchase. For a business, this becomes very important as this might make or break their business. Understanding the consumer segment (positive or negative) of their product or service is key so that they can try to react at the earliest to sustain the service to their consumer base.

5. In the airline industry logistic regression is heavily used to understand whether a customer will purchase an in-flight meal or is likely to upgrade to business class for a small fee during a 4+ hour flight and so on. This happens specifically in low-cost airlines.

The Sigmoid function

The binary classification starts with the sigmoid function, which depicts the probability of the function. The closer the value of the function is to 1, the higher the propensity for it to be labelled as category 1 otherwise labelled as category 0.

$$P = \frac{e^{\beta_0 + \beta_1 X_1}}{1 + e^{\beta_0 + \beta_1 X_1}}$$

The logistic regression coefficient associated with the predictor variable determines the per unit change based on a unit change in X_1. This S-shaped sigmoid function asymptotes between 0 and 1 and depicts the probability of an event happening. This function can be extended when there is more than one covariate, which is often the case in many industrial applications today.

$$P = \frac{e^{\beta_0 + \beta_1 X_1 + \beta_2 X_2 + \cdots \beta_n X_n}}{1 + e^{\beta_0 + \beta_1 X_1 + \beta_2 X_2 + \cdots \beta_n X_n}}$$

An interesting transformation of the above is applying a logit transformation on the probability P of an event with all the covariates X. The transformation results in a simple linear regression and the bounds from 0 to1 changed to $-\infty$ to ∞.

$$\text{logit}(P) = \beta_0 + \beta_1 X_1 + \beta_2 X_2 + \cdots \beta_n X_n$$

Interpreting the coefficients

Consider an example where a bank wants to build a product that classifies whether a customer will pay his/her credit card bill on time or not, provided some information about the customer is available. Assume no information about the customer is available. The product is queried to classify customer data and indicate if the customer will pay his/her credit card bill on time. This would amount to setting all the covariates X in the model to 0, and if the model is assumed to be unbiased then together with all β coefficients, β_0 also assumes 0. The sigmoid function reduces to:

$$P = \frac{e^0}{1 + e^0} = \frac{1}{2} = 0.5$$

Thus, without any information, an unbiased system is unable to take any decision. This is as good as tossing a coin, as there is a 50 per cent chance the customer may fail to pay his/her bill on time. If there is evidence of a biased situation and the history suggests there are instances of many delayed payments, and no information about the customer is available, then all covariates X are set to 0, with β_0 assuming a value of 2 (due to delayed payments, and estimated as part of a model building), and the sigmoid function reduces to:

$$P = \frac{e^2}{1 + e^2} = 0.88$$

Here it can be said that there is an 88 per cent chance that a randomly chosen customer will not pay his/her credit card bill on time.

Example

ABC airlines is a low-cost airline known for its economical fares to destinations in the EU. As part of its marketing strategy, the airline deploys multiple campaigns to boost revenue by offering customers value-added services for a small additional charge such as travel insurance, in-flight meals, additional baggage allowance, seat selection, seats with extra legroom, airport pick up/drop off, etc. Customers who purchase these add-on services boost the company's top line key performance indicators (KPIs). Thus, it is of interest to see how the airline can optimize the same. This is important as the marketing team may want to know how many meals are guaranteed to sell and how many may be estimated as impromptu purchases so they can plan the purchase of fresh stock. Using a snapshot of customer data encompassing their psychographic, transactional and demographic profiles, a logistic regression model is built to understand if a customer is likely to purchase an in-flight meal if advertized through an appropriate marketing campaign (e.g., an e-mail campaign). For a business, the objective is to identify those customers who are likely to purchase a service if targeted with an appropriate e-mail campaign.

Model evaluation

Building a logistic regression model and estimating the coefficients can be done using any software or openly available tools like R, MATLAB, Julia, or Python. The goal is to understand and evaluate the model for business decision-making. Say from the snapshot of customer data of over 50,000 travellers in the past quarter, it is observed that only about 15 per cent of these customers have purchased an in-flight meal (pre-booked). To understand the customer motivation or intent, it is important to select the right metrics that enable one to know if a good model has been built that can answer business questions of interest. Suppose a sample of data (say, 50,000 records) is taken and split in the ratio of 70:30 for training and test data sets to see how well the model performs. With the visibility of the actual data, the interest is to know if a customer purchases a meal plan or not. A simple and common way to understand the model is by constructing a confusion matrix.

A confusion matrix is a simple and powerful tool that allows one to visualize and understand how good the model is.

	Predicted by the model as 1	Predicted by the model as 0	
True 1	True positive (TP)	False negative (FN)	Recall TP/(TP+FN)
True 0	False positive (FP)	True negative (TN)	
	Precision TP/(TP+FP)		Accuracy (TP+TN)/(TP+FP+TN+FN)

In addition to the accuracy with which the model correctly predicted a purchase or not, there are a few other metrics that are helpful in various business situations. The four basic metrics as shown in the above confusion matrix table are:

1. True positives (TP): The number of records that are correctly identified as positive. In the example, the number of times the model detected a customer will purchase an in-flight meal when the customer purchased an in-flight meal.
2. True negatives (TN): The number of records that are correctly identified as negative. In the example, the number of times the model detected a customer will not purchase an in-flight meal when the customer did not purchase an in-flight meal.
3. False positives (FP): The number of records that are incorrectly identified as positive. In the example, the number of times the model detected a customer will purchase an in-flight meal when the customer did not purchase an in-flight meal.
4. False negatives (FN): The number of records that are incorrectly identified as negative. In the example, the number of times the model detected a customer will not purchase an in-flight meal when the customer purchased an in-flight meal.

In the example, the 50,000 travellers' data can be classified into a confusion matrix as:

	Predicted by the model as 1	Predicted by the model as 0	
True 1	3405	112	0.9681
True 0	1340	45143	
	0.7176		0.9709

Using a 0.5 probability cut-off, the model has an accuracy of 97 per cent. One key aspect that can be noticed is that in this problem, the conversion rate is under 15 per cent. This means that less than 15 per cent of customers purchase an in-flight meal. This also means that there is an imbalance in the customers buying in-flight meal and customers not buying in-flight meal. The number of records of people not purchasing an in-flight meal is more than thirteen times that of the customers purchasing an in-flight meal. In such situations, looking at accuracy itself as a sole metric will lead to false decisions.

Consider a situation in which a created model detected no true positives at all, or the model predicted all cases as true negatives or transfer the true positives to any other class. Then the confusion matrix will look as follows:

	Predicted by the model as 1	Predicted by the model as 0	
True 1	0	3512	0
True 0	1345	45143	
	0		0.9028

Notice that if a model classifies all records as 0 (that is, no customer purchased an in-flight meal), the model ends up with an accuracy of over 90 per cent. What happened to precision and recall?

The two important derived metrics are:

1. Precision: The ratio of correctly predicted positive class to all the records predicted as positive. In the example, it is the number of records where the model predicted that the customer would purchase an in-flight meal when the customer actually may or may not have purchased a meal.

2. Recall: The ratio of correctly predicted positive class to all the positive records. In the example, it is the number of records where the model predicted that the customer would purchase an in-flight meal when the customer purchased the in-flight meal.

Precision and recall are important metrics that show how the classifier has been designed. In the above example, not detecting a positive class, having a high accuracy rate, with zero precision and zero recall leads to suspicion of the functioning of the model and needs a closer look. Precision is significant when false positives are more important than false negatives. In the case of the example here, precision is not that crucial. The company needs to target customers who are not likely to purchase an in-flight meal. Recall is significant when false negatives are more important than false positives. In the case of the example, here it is important for the company to have a higher recall or can detect all customers who are likely to purchase an in-flight meal.

The ideal situation is to have a model that has high accuracy, precision and recall. Since such an ideal situation doesn't exist, the model that better serves the business is selected by appropriately choosing the metrics. Precision and recall are key metrics that show how a model is performing on the edge cases if it is leaning towards false positives or false negatives. These two metrics can be combined into a single metric, known as the F1 score. The F1 score is the weighted average of precision and recall.

$$F1 = \frac{2(\text{ Precision } \times \text{ Recall})}{\text{Precision } + \text{ Recall}}$$

The F1 score takes a value between 0 and 1. Similar to the correlation coefficient, an F1 score closer to 1 means an ideal performance of classifying correctly, and an F1 score closer to 0 means the model predictions are poor. Only when both precision and recall perform well will the F1 score have a higher value. Thus, this becomes a more powerful metric than accuracy alone.

In the example, at a 0.5 probability cut-off the system was in favour of false positives. The F1 score is

$$F1 = \frac{2(\text{Precision } \times \text{ Recall})}{\text{Precision } + \text{ Recall}} = \frac{2 \times 0.7176 \times 0.9681}{0.7176 \times 0.9681} = 0.8242$$

A desirable way to build a classifier model is to predict the probability over the Sigmoid function and tag each row of data as 1 if the probability is greater than 0.5, or 0 otherwise. This approach may not be an ideal case most of the time. The figure below shows the distribution of the probabilities of the record to be either 1 (a customer purchases an in-flight meal) or 0 (a customer doesn't purchase an in-flight meal). The idea of building a good binary classifier is to ensure that the separation of these two distributions is clear and falls as far away from each other as possible. That ideal scenario never happens in real life. One way to improve the logistic regression model is to select the point of intersection of these two distributions as the cut-off point to choose whether the consumer record favours a purchase or not. When the cut-off probability is 0.70, a larger separation between the two classes is observed. To simplify the comprehension, usually, density estimation is used to estimate the probabilities of a continuous random variable instead of a histogram with larger bins to visualize the distributions smoothly.

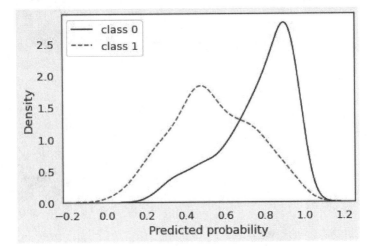

Given the above (using the cut-off probability of 0.70), the consumer metrics can be reconstructed as follows.

	Predicted by the model as 1	Predicted by the model as 0	
True 1	3777	343	0.9167
True 0	768	45112	
	0.8310		0.9778

The F1 score is

$$F1 = \frac{2(\text{Precision} \times \text{Recall})}{\text{Precision} + \text{Recall}} = \frac{2 \times 0.8310 \times 0.9167}{0.8310 \times 0.9167} = 0.8717$$

This clearly shows a simple way to look at metrics that are more relevant to choosing what is of interest in a study and identify model biases and how to overcome the same. In some business situations, a specific metric will be more important than the other/s. For example, during the current pandemic, the interest would be to detect all COVID positive cases as positive and keep false negatives as small as possible. Technically, it may not be dangerous to classify some non-COVID cases as positive as it is not as risky as classifying a COVID positive case as negative.